1201 Quotes for Winners

That help you Excel in Business and Life

By

Hitesh Changela

Dedication

To all men and women quoted in this book,

Whose words have inspired countless and will continue to
do so for generations to come...

Your <u>Free</u> Gift

Build Your Action Plan
To excel in business and life

Action brings results! So I have created a special action plan for readers to help them achieving excellence in business and life.

To grab your action plan, go to
http://www.hiteshchangela.com/actionplan

Contents

Introduction

Quotes have always fascinated me since my MBA pursuit in marketing 20 years ago. Quotes have given and continue to give me instant wisdom, insight and motivation.

We are living in an age of struggle, constantly trying to maintain a balance between our personal and professional lives.

We need constant inspiration, motivation and words of wisdom to help us overcome challenging situations.

This book is a compilation of quotes from 551 world's most successful men and women who have provided a great service in helping humankind by sharing their life experiences through a short few words or sentences. Each hand-picked quote is insightful, inspirational and uplifting.

We all have dark moments in life when we have self-doubt or we feel all hope is lost and desperately looking for help.

Allow these timeless words to inspire you. Listen to them. Take their guidance and act on them.

I hope you will find this book useful. Your suggestions and feedback are most welcome. Please send an email to quotes@hiteshchangela.com

Hitesh Changela
CEO, Author, Entrepreneur
London, July 2016

Getting the most out of this book

Here are suggestions on how to get results from this book:

1. This book doesn't follow a logical sequence. You can read a book from beginning to end or choose a category or topic which best suits your particular needs.
2. Highlight quotes which you feel best help you at a particular moment in your life.
3. Index by the author gives you a quote number for each author.
4. Index by category gives you a range of quote numbers for each category.
5. Keep this book handy and read it numerous times, each time you will get different insights.
6. Recommend or send this book as a surprise gift to help your beloved family, friends, business colleagues or whosoever might benefit from it.
7. The action is critical; nothing happens until you become proactive and take action.

Note:

These quotes have been gathered from numerous sources and every care has been taken to attribute quotes to the right person, however, in some cases it is almost impossible to find who the original author is. Also, sometimes quotes are incorrectly assigned to famous individuals to make them more memorable.

When a quote has multiple deviations, I have chosen quotes which I feel best fit the overall aim of this book.

1. Action

1
If not us, who? If not now, when?
Hillel the Elder

2
Every morning in Africa, a gazelle wakes up, it knows it must outrun the fastest lion or it will be killed. Every morning in Africa, a lion wakes up. It knows it must run faster than the slowest gazelle, or it will starve. It doesn't matter whether you're the lion or a gazelle - when the sun comes up, you'd better be running.
Christopher McDougall

3
If you can't fly then run, if you can't run then walk, if you can't walk then crawl, but whatever you do you have to keep moving forward.
Martin Luther King, Jr.

4
Your first step is all that it takes to reach success. It shows your faith in your dreams. It shows you belief in yourself. It shows you have courage to move ahead.
Unknown

5

In any moment of decision, the best thing you can do is the right thing, the next best thing is the wrong thing, and the worst thing you can do is nothing.
Theodore Roosevelt

6

The best time to plant a tree was 20 years ago. The second best time is now.
Chinese Proverb

7

The value of an idea lies in the using of it.
Thomas A. Edison

8

You see in life lots of people know what to do, but few people actually do what they know. Knowing is not enough! You must take action.
Tony Robbins

9

Do something now, that will make the person you'll be tomorrow, proud to have been the person you are today.
Unknown

10

Sometimes the smallest step in the right direction ends up being the biggest step of your life. Tip toe if you must, but take the step.
Naeem Callaway

11

Dream Big. Start small. Act now.
Robin Sharma

12

Words can inspire, thoughts can provoke, but only action truly
brings you closer to your dreams.
Brad Sugars

13

If you act enthusiastic, you'll be enthusiastic!
Dale Carnegie

14

Action conquers fear.
Peter Nivio Zarlenga

15

Try not. Do, or do not. There is no try.
Yoda

16

Well done is better than well said.
Benjamin Franklin

17

Do it now. Sometimes `later' becomes `never.'
Unknown

18

A year from now you may wish you had started today.
Karen Lamb

19
What you do speaks so loudly that I cannot hear what you say.
Ralph Waldo Emerson

20
If you talk about it, it's a dream, if you envision it, it's possible, but if you schedule it, it's real.
Tony Robbins

21
The secret of getting ahead is getting started.
Mark Twain

22
It is not necessary to do extraordinary things to get extraordinary results.
Warren Buffett

23
Doubt increases with inaction. Clarity reveals itself in momentum. Growth comes from progress. For all these reasons, BEGIN.
Brendon Burchard

24
You don't have to be great to start but you have to START to be great.
Zig Ziglar

25
The few who do are the envy of the many who only watch.
Jim Rohn

26
Action is the foundational key to all success.
Pablo Picasso

27
The way to get started is to quit talking and begin doing.
Walt Disney

28
You can't cross the sea merely by standing and staring at the water.
Rabindranath Tagore

29
It's better to do something for nothing than nothing for nothing.
Patricia Fripp

30
An ounce of performance is worth pounds of promises.
Mae West

31
Done is better than perfect.
Sheryl Sandberg

32
A journey of a thousand miles begins with a single step.
Lao Tzu

33
Don't wait. The time will never be just right.
Napoleon Hill

34
Don't stay in bed unless you make money in bed.
George Burns

35
Take action every day - some small dose at a time.
Jeffrey Gitomer

36
Trying is winning in the moment.
Dan Waldschmidt

37
Always do your best. What you plant now, you will harvest later.
Og Mandino

38
Do more than just talk; act. Do more than just promise; deliver.
Steve Maraboli

39
Choices are at the root of every one of your results. Each choice
starts a behavior that over time becomes a habit.
Darren Hardy

40

It's impossible, said pride. It's risky, said experiences. It's pointless, said reason. Give it a try, whispered the HEART.
Unknown

41

It's pretty simple - The Action you take will determine the results you Achieve.
Tony Robbins

42

You could make a wish or you could make it happen.
Unknown

43

Leaving your comfort zone is hard. Staying broke is hard. Pick your hard.
Unknown

44

The miracle of the seed and the soil is not available by affirmation; it is only available by labor.
Jim Rohn

45

Day by day, what you do is who you become.
Heraclitus

46

Great thoughts speak only to the thoughtful mind, but great actions speak to all mankind.
Emily P. Bissell

47

If you want to make your dreams come true, the first thing you
have to do is wake up.
J. M. Power

48

If you never try you'll never know.
Unknown

49

Stop waiting for things to happen. Go out and make them
happen.
Unknown

50

Begin somewhere; you cannot build a reputation on what you
intend to do.
Li Smith

51

You miss 100% of the shots you don't take.
Wayne Gretzky

52

If we wait for the moment when everything, absolutely
everything is ready, we shall never begin.
Ivan Turgenev

53

The pessimist complains about the wind; the optimist expects it
to change; the realist adjusts the sails.
William Arthur Ward

54
The formula for successful customer service has been discovered. So has the formula for reducing the risk of heart attack. They have the same problem - Only one in twenty who know the formula will do anything about it. Knowing and doing are two different worlds.
Jeffrey Gitomer

55
A good plan, violently executed now, is better than a perfect plan next week.
General George Patton

56
Someday is not a day of the week.
Denise Brennan-Nelson

57
It is not what you say, or wish, or hope or intend, it is only what you do that counts.
Brian Tracy

58
Luck favors those in motion.
General George Patton

59
Start where you are. Use what you have. Do what you can.
Arthur Ashe

60
Do you want to know who you are? Don't ask. Act! Action will delineate and define you.
Thomas Jefferson

61
All glory comes from daring to begin.
Eugene F. Ware

62
You can't build a reputation on what you are going to do.
Henry Ford

63
If you want something you've never had, then you've got to do something you've never done.
Thomas Jefferson

64
The best preparation for tomorrow is to do today's work superbly well.
William Osler

65
Things may come to those who wait, but only the things left by those who hustle.
Abraham Lincoln

66
If something is important enough, even if the odds are against you, you should still do it.
Elon Musk

67
While you are still waiting to find an easy way (or a perfect time), someone else is already getting results because they decided making progress is more important than making excuses.
Unknown

68
The path to success is to take massive, determined action.
Tony Robbins

69
What you do today can improve all your tomorrows.
Ralph Marston

70
The man who removes a mountain begins by carrying away small stones.
Chinese Proverb

71
Do not wait to strike till the iron is hot; but make it hot by striking.
William Butler Yeats

2. Attitude

72
Excellence is not a skill. It's an attitude.
Ralph Marston

73
Your attitude, not your aptitude, will determine your altitude.
Zig Ziglar

74
The problem is not the problem. The problem is your attitude about the problem.
Captain Jack Sparrow

75
I cannot give you the formula for success, but I can give you the formula for failure - which is, "Try to please everybody."
Herbert Bayard Swope

76
I have no special talent. I am only passionately curious.
Albert Einstein

77
A great attitude becomes a great day which becomes a great month which becomes a great year which becomes a great LIFE.
Mandy Hale

78
Stress and unhappiness come not from situations, but how you respond to situations.
Brian Tracy

79
Everyone may not be good, but there's always something good in everyone. Never judge anyone shortly because every saint has a past and every sinner has a future.
Oscar Wilde

80
Be humble you could be wrong.
Unknown

81
Sooner or later those who win are those who think they can.
Paul Tournier

82
Go the extra mile it's never crowded.
Unknown

83
If you want to be paid more, promoted faster, or increase your earning ability, you have to increase the value of the work that you do.
Brian Tracy

84
Your smile will give you a positive countenance that will make people feel comfortable around you.
Les Brown

85
There is no future in any job. The future lies in the man who holds the job.
George W. Crane

86
Don't stress the could haves. If it should have, it would have.
Unknown

87
Paying attention to simple little things that most men neglect makes a few men rich.
Henry Ford

88
Never neglect the little things. Never skimp on that extra effort, that additional few minutes, that soft word of praise or thanks, that delivery of the very best that you can do. It does not matter what others think, it is of prime importance, however, what you think about you. You can never do your best, which should always be your trademark, if you are cutting corners and shirking responsibilities. You are special. Act it. Never neglect the little things.
Og Mandino

89

No excuses. No explanations. You don't win on emotion. You win on execution.
Tony Dungy

90

Yesterday I was clever, so I wanted to change the world. Today I am wise, so I am changing myself.
Rumi

91

If you're not prepared to be wrong, you'll never come up with anything original.
Ken Robinson

92

You can't have a million dollar dream with a minimum wage worth ethic.
Zig Ziglar

93

The optimist sees opportunity in every danger; the pessimist sees danger in every opportunity.
Winston Churchill

94

WORRYING does not take away tomorrow's TROUBLES, it takes away today's PEACE.
Zig Ziglar

95
Big pay and little responsibility are circumstances seldom found together.
Napoleon Hill

96
Surrender to what is. Let go of what was. Have faith in what will be.
Sonia Ricotti

97
Lack of planning on your part does not constitute an emergency on my part.
Unknown

98
I will love the light for it shows me the way, yet I will endure the darkness because it shows me the stars.
Og Mandino

99
You have to do more than you get paid for because that's where the fortune is.
Jim Rohn

100
Get comfortable with the uncomfortable.
Jillian Michael

101

When you wake up every day, you have two choices. You can either be positive or negative; an optimist or a pessimist. I choose to be an optimist. It's all a matter of perspective.
Harvey Mackay

102

How you think when you lose determines how long it will be until you win.
Gilbert K. Chesterton

103

Attitude precedes service. Your positive mental attitude is the basis for the way you act and react to people. 'You become what you think about' is the foundation of your actions and reactions. What are your thoughts? Positive all the time? How are you guiding them?"
Jeffrey Gitomer

3. Business

104
Work on your business. Not in your business.
Michael Gerber

105
To be successful, you have to have your heart in your business,
and your business in your heart.
Sr. Thomas Watson

106
Businesses succeed because of high sales; businesses fail because
of low sales. All else is commentary.
Brian Tracy

107
Boil down your strategy in to one simple promise - and that
promise should be important and unique.
David Ogilvy

108
Technology is nothing. What's important is that you have a faith
in people, that they're basically good and smart, and if you give
them tools, they'll do wonderful things with them.
Steve Jobs

109

In the end, all business operations can be reduced to three words; people, product and profits. Unless you've got a good team, you can't do much with the other two.
Lee Iacocca

110

If you don't have competitive advantage, don't compete.
Jack Welch

111

You don't build a business. You build people and then people build the business.
Zig Ziglar

112

There is only one winning strategy. It is to carefully define the target market and direct a superior offering to that target market.
Philip Kotler

113

Your big opportunity may be right where you are now.
Napoleon Hill

114

The ability to find a customer, sell your product or service to that customer, and satisfy the customer so that he buys from you again should be the central focus of all entrepreneurial activity.
Brian Tracy

115

Somebody, somewhere can always do something similar cheaper. But think about yourself: Most people generally don't buy features. They buy what they feel gives them the most value for a specific solution.
Monika D'Agostino

116

A man without a smiling face must not open a shop.
Chinese Proverb

117

You can't expect to meet the challenges of today with yesterday's tools and expect to be in business tomorrow.
Unknown

118

Do not hire a man who does your work for money, but him who does it for love of it.
Henry David Thoreau

119

The aim of marketing is to know and understand the customer so well that the product or service fits him and sells itself.
Peter F. Drucker

120

In God we trust, all others bring data.
W. Edwards Deming

121

Fish where the fish are.
Axiom for salespeople

122

Half the money I spend on advertising is wasted, and the trouble is, I don't know which half.
John Wanamaker

123

Customers will never love a company until the employees love it first.
Simon Sinek

124

Our business is not to casually please everyone, but to deeply please our target customers.
Philip Kotler

125

Marketing begins before the product is launched.
Seth Godin

126

Innovation is not about saying yes to everything. It's about saying NO to all but the most crucial features.
Steve Jobs

127

Understanding and building great relationships are part of the foundation of any great business and industry.
Peter Borders

128
When you innovate, you've got to be prepared for everyone
telling you you're nuts.
Larry Ellison

129
Marketing is not a battle of products, it's a battle of perceptions.
Al Ries and Jack Trout

130
Marketing is no longer about the stuff that you make, but about
the stories you tell.
Seth Godin

131
Never do a good deal with a bad guy.
Zig Ziglar

132
A product for everyone rarely reaches much of anyone.
Seth Godin

133
Know your numbers' is a fundamental precept of business.
Bill Gates

134
Branding is what people say about you when you are not in the
room.
Jeff Bezos

135
All business success rests on something labeled a sale, which at least momentarily weds company and customer.
Tom Peter

136
For small business people, less paperwork means higher profits, boosted sales and more time with the family.
Tony Abbott

137
We watch our competitors, learn from them, see the things that they were doing for customers and copy those things as much as we can.
Jeff Bezos

138
The most powerful concept in marketing is owning a word in the prospect's mind.
Al Ries and Jack Trout

139
It has been a founding principle of our company to listen to the end-users, the consumers, and not just guess what they want.
Montgomery Kersten

140
5 Essentials for small business owners:
1. **Marketing** - Everything you do to attract prospects to your business.
2. **Sales** - Everything you do to convert prospects into paying customers.
3. **Operations** - Everything you do to serve your clients.
4. **Administration** - Everything you do to track your numbers and the internal office systems to the business.
5. **Leadership** - Everything you do to lead and guide your business.
Howard Partridge

141
A brand is no longer what we tell consumer it is - it is what consumers tell each other it is.
Scott Cook

142
You cannot innovate by copying.
Larry Ellison

143
Information is the lifeblood of business, and software is what gives people and businesses the ability to harness it.
It enables companies to constantly hone their competitive edge.
Steve Ballmer

144
If you can't describe what you are doing as a process, you don't know what you're doing.
W. Edwards Deming

145
My ability to tell a better story than my competitors became the
reason we had a successful company.
Gary Vaynerchuk

146
How you gather, manage and use information will determine
whether you win or lose.
Bill Gates

147
Surround yourself with the best people you can find, delegate
authority, and don't interfere as long as the policy you've decided
upon is being carried out.
Ronald Reagan

148
It's not about having the right opportunities. It's about handling
the opportunities right.
Mark Hunter

149
Work expands to fill the time available for its completion.
Cyril Northcote Parkinson.

150
It used to be that people needed products to survive. Now
products need people to survive.
Nicholas Johnson

151
Every organization has to prepare for the abandonment of everything it does.
Peter F. Drucker

152
Quality is the best business plan.
John Lasseter

153
Pay attention to your enemies, for they are the first to discover your mistakes.
Antisthenes

154
Before you build a better mousetrap, it helps to know if there are any mice out there.
Mortimer Zuckerman

155
Quality is remembered long after price is forgotten.
Aldo Gucci

156
Your smile is your logo, your personality is your business card, how you leave others feeling after having an experience with you becomes your trademark.
Jay Danzie

157

It's better to be first in the mind than to be first in the marketplace.
Al Ries and Jack Trout

158

In the future, it will become increasingly obvious that your competitors are just as clueless as you are.
Scott Adams

159

Your ability to clearly define and determine the very best customer for your product or service will determine your success in business.
Brian Tracy

160

A brand for a company is like a reputation for a person. You earn reputation by trying to do hard things well.
Jeff Bezos

4. Challenge, Setback & Mistake

161
We are continually faced with a series of great opportunities
brilliantly disguised as insoluble problems.
Lee Iacocca

162
If I had to live my life again, I'd make the same mistakes, only
sooner.
Tallulah Bankhead

163
One thing is certain in business: you will make mistakes. When
you are pushing the boundaries, mistakes are inevitable - how
you react is important.
Richard Branson

164
The harder the conflict, the more glorious the triumph.
Thomas Paine

165
What to do with a mistake - recognize it, admit it, learn from it,
forget it.
Dean Smith

166
There are plenty of difficult obstacles in your path. Don't allow
yourself to become one of them.
Ralph Marston

167
If you learn from defeat, you haven't really lost.
Zig Ziglar

168
If you have a setback in life, think of yourself as a rubber band:
The further back you go, the more POWER you have to spring
forward.
Unknown

169
A setback is a setup for a comeback.
T.D. Jakes

170
The significant problems we face cannot be solved at the same
level of thinking we were at when we created them.
Albert Einstein

171
Never tell your problems to anyone . . . 20% don't care and the
other 80% are glad you have them.
Lou Holtz

172
Constant effort and frequent mistakes are the stepping
stones to genius.
Elbert Hubbard

173
In the middle of a difficulty lies opportunity.
Albert Einstein

174
Never get too hung up on mistakes.
Warren Buffett

175
It's not how we make mistakes, but how we correct them that
defines us.
Unknown

176
Anyone who has never made a mistake has never tried anything
new.
Albert Einstein

177
Success does not consist in never making mistakes but in never
making the same one a second time.
George Bernard Shaw

178
Our mistakes won't irreparably damage our lives unless we let
them.
James E Sweeney

179
Originality and a feeling of one's own dignity are achieved only
through work and struggle.
Fyodor Dostoevsky

180
Make mistakes faster.
Andy Grove

181
An obstacle is often a stepping stone.
William Prescott

182
A rejection is nothing more than a necessary step in the pursuit
of success.
Bo Bennett

183
Man needs difficulties in life because they are necessary to enjoy
the success.
A.P.J. Abdul Kalam

184
Whenever you make a mistake or get knocked down by life, don't
look back at it too long. Mistakes are life's way of teaching you.
Your capacity for occasional blunders is inseparable from your
capacity to reach your goals. No one wins them all, and your
failures, when they happen, are just part of your growth. Shake
off your blunders. How will you know your limits without an
occasional failure? Never quit. Your turn will come.
Og Mandino

185
The difficulties you will meet will resolve themselves as you
advance.
Jim Rohn

186
Challenges are what make life interest; overcoming them is what makes life meaningful.
Joshua J. Marine

187
A smooth sea never made a skilled sailor.
Proverbs

188
Mistakes are proof that you are trying.
Unknown

189
Don't let the mistakes and disappointments of the past control and direct your future.
Zig Ziglar

190
Obstacles are those frightful things you see when you take your eyes off the goal.
Henry Ford

191
Obstacles are necessary for success because in selling, as in all careers of importance, victory comes only after many struggles and countless defeats.
Og Mandino

192
When you focus on POSSIBILITIES instead of PROBLEMS...You will see more OPPORTUNITIES in your life!
Unknown

5. Change

193
If you don't like where you are, then change it. You are not a tree.
Jim Rohn

194
Change before you have to.
Jack Welch

195
Growth is painful. Change is painful. But nothing is as painful as staying stuck somewhere you don't belong.
Mandy Hale

196
The world hates change, yet it is the only thing that has brought progress.
Charles Kettering

197
If it doesn't challenge you, it won't change you.
Fred DeVito

198
Welcome to today. Another day, another chance. Feel free to change.
Unknown

199
Nothing endures but change.
Heraclitus

200
I am convinced that if the rate of change inside an organization is less than the rate of change outside, the end is in sight.
Jack Welch

201
What got you here won't get you there.
Marshall Goldsmith

202
Your life does not get better by chance, it gets better by change!
Jim Rohn

203
Don't complain about things you're not willing to change.
Unknown

204
You cannot control what happens to you, but you can control your attitude toward what happens to you, and if that, you will be mastering change rather than allowing to master you.
Brian Tracy

205
Those who are victorious plan effectively and change decisively.
Sun Tzu

206
The majority of men meet with failure because of their lack of persistence in creating new plans to take the place of those which fail.
Napoleon Hill

207
If today were the last day of my life, would I want to do what I am about to do today?" And whenever the answer has been "No" for too many days in a row, I know I need to change something.
Steve Jobs

208
When you blame others, you give up your power to change.
Robert Anthony

6. Character & Integrity

209
Character, in the long run, is the decisive factor in the life of an individual and of nations alike.
Theodore Roosevelt

210
Sow a thought, reap an action; sow an action, reap a habit; sow a habit, reap a character; sow a character, reap a destiny.
Unknown

211
It takes 20 years to build a reputation and five minutes to ruin it. If you think about that, you'll do things differently.
Warren Buffett

212
Happiness is when what you think, what you say, and what you do are in harmony.
Mahatma Gandhi

213
You can easily judge the character of a man by how he treats those who can do nothing for him.
Malcolm Forbes

214

One man cannot do right in one department of life whilst he is occupied in doing wrong in any other department. Life is one indivisible whole.
Mahatma Gandhi

215

No change of circumstances can repair a defect of character.
Ralph Waldo Emerson

216

Nearly all men can stand adversity, but if you want to test a man's character, give him power.
Abraham Lincoln

217

Key to many is one. i.e. how you regard one is often reflects how you regards other.
Stephen Covey

218

I believe in the sacredness of a promise, that a man's word should be as good as his bond; that character - not wealth or power or position - is of supreme worth.
John D. Rockefeller (Jr.)

219

Live in harmony with your highest values and your innermost convictions. Never compromise.
Brian Tracy

220
Whatever you are, be a good one.
Abraham Lincoln

221
Money doesn't make us anyway it just unmasks us.
Henry Ford

222
Integrity is choosing your thoughts and actions based on values
rather than personal gains.
Unknown

223
The ultimate measure of a man is not where he stands in
moments of comfort and convenience, but where he stands at
times of challenge and controversy.
Martin Luther King, Jr.

224
Strive not to be success, but rather to be of value.
Albert Einstein

225
The supreme quality for leadership is unquestionably integrity.
Without it, no real success is possible, no matter whether it is on
a section gang, a football field, in an army, or in an office.
Dwight Eisenhower

226
Be more concerned with your character than your reputation, because your character is what you really are, while your reputation is merely what others think you are.
John Wooden

227
You can't fool all the people, not even most of the time. People, once unfooled, talk about the experience.
Seth Godin

228
Trust is the foundation of every relationship. Never compromise your ability to build & maintain trust.
Miles Austin

229
Instead of trying to sound interesting to others, be interested in them.
Brain J. Carroll

230
Character is the salesperson's stock-intrade. The product itself is secondary. Truthfulness, enthusiasm and patience are gre at assets to every salesperson. Without them, they couldn't go far. Courage and courtesy are essential equipment.
George M. Adams

231
The more real and transparent you are with people, the more real and transparent they will be with you.
John Barrows

232
Character may be manifested in the great moments, but it is
made in the small ones.
Phillips Brooks

233
The most important persuasion tool you have in your entire
arsenal is integrity.
Zig Ziglar

234
If people like you, they'll listen to you, but if they trust you,
they'll do business with you.
Zig Ziglar

235
Whatever good things we build end up building us.
Jim Rohn

236
To give real service you must add something which cannot be
bought or measured with money, and that is sincerity and
integrity.
Douglas Adams

237
There can be no friendship without confidence, and no
confidence without integrity.
Samuel Johnson

238
The superior man understands what is right; the inferior man understands what will sell.
Confucius

239
Integrity is what we do, what we say, and what we say we do.
Don Galer

240
To be trusted is a greater compliment than to be loved.
George MacDonald

7. Courage

241
Whatever you can do, or dream you can, begin it. Boldness has genius, power and magic in it. Begin it now.
Johann Wolfgang Goethe

242
Whatever you do, you need courage.
Ralph Waldo Emerson

243
Life shrinks or expands in proportion to one's courage.
Anaïs Nin

244
Courage is contagious. When a brave man takes a stand, the spines of others are often stiffened.
Billy Graham

245
I'd rather die on my feet, than live upon my knees.
Emiliano Zapata

246
Courage conquers all things.
Ovid

247
Whenever you see a successful business, someone once made a
courageous decision.
Peter F. Drucker

248
Challenge yourself with something you know you could never do,
and what you'll find is that you can overcome anything.
Unknown

249
It is not because things are difficult that we do not dare; it is
because we do not dare that things are difficult.
Seneca

250
Fearlessness is not the absence of fear. It's the mastery of fear. It's
about getting up one more time than we fall down.
Arianna Huffington

251
Brave men may not live forever, but cautious men do not live at
all.
Unknown

252
If you are always trying to be normal, you will never know how
amazing you can be.
Maya Angelou

253
If we all did the things we are capable of doing, we would literally astound ourselves.
Thomas A. Edison

254
Success is never final. Failure is never fatal. It is courage that counts.
Winston Churchill

255
One does not discover new lands without consenting to lose sight of the shore for a very long time.
André Gide

256
Any intelligent fool can make things bigger, more complex and more violent. It takes a touch of genius and a lot of courage to move in the opposite direction.
Ernst Schumacher

257
Fortune favours the bold.
Virgil

258
When life gives you something that makes you feel afraid, that's when life gives you a chance to be brave.
Lupytha Hermin

259
Sometimes all you need is twenty seconds of insane courage. Just literally twenty seconds of just embarrassing bravery and I promise you, something great will come of it.
Benjamin Mee

260
Strength doesn't come from what you can do. It comes from overcoming the things you once thought you couldn't.
Rikki Rogers

261
Be brave, take risks, nothing can substitute experience.
Paulo Coelho

262
Every time we've moved ahead in IBM, it was because someone was willing to take a chance, put his head on the block, and try something new.
Thomas J. Watson

263
Greatness is not measured by money and stature, it is measured by courage and heart.
Unknown

8. Customer

264
The purpose of business is to create and keep a customer.
Peter F. Drucker

265
Your success ultimately depends on what you have contributed to the success of your customers.
Peter F. Drucker

266
A customer is the most important visitor on our premises. He is not dependent on us. We are dependent on him. He is not an interruption on our work. He is the purpose of it. He is not an outsider on our business. He is a part of it. We are not doing him a favour by serving him. He is doing us a favour by giving us an opportunity to do so.
Mahatma Gandhi

267
Is the purpose of a customer to get a sale or is the purpose of a sale to get a customer?
Chris Cardell

268
The only profit centre is the customer. Everything else is the cost in the business.
Peter F. Drucker

269
Everything starts with the customer.
June Martin

270
We've entered the age of the customer. We believe we are at the beginning of a 20 year business cycle in which the most successful enterprises will reinvent themselves to systematically serve their customers.
Sheryl Pattek

271
A satisfied customer is the best business strategy of all.
Michael LeBoeuf

272
There is only one boss. The customer. And he can fire everybody in the company from
the chairman on down, simply by spending his money somewhere else.
Sam Walton

273
Make a customer, not a sale.
Katherine Barchetti

274
You've got to start with the customer experience and work backwards to the technology.
Steve Jobs

275
Think like a customer.
Paul Gillin

276
We built this company from the customer back, not from the
company out.
Lou Gerstner

277
We see our customers as invited guests to a party, and we are the
hosts. It's our job every day to make every important aspect of the
customer experience a little bit better.
Jeff Bezos

278
New customers come from the actions of past customers.
Eric Ries

279
Nobody can guarantee your job. Only customers can guarantee
your job.
Philip Kotler

280
When things aren't going well, call your best
customer...someone you have helped.
Mark Hunter

281
Your best customers leave quite an impression. Do the same, and
they won't leave at all.
SAP Ad

282

Make the customer the hero of your story.
Ann Handley

283

Focus on having the maximum impact in every client interaction.
It takes more time to prepare, but it pays off big time.
Jill Konrath

284

Use your CRM to retain customers.
Jeffrey Gitomer

285

Use testimonial letters from satisfied customers at every
opportunity.
Brian Tracy

286

To satisfy our customers' needs, we'll give them what they want,
not what we want to give them.
Steve James

287

The golden rule for every businessman is this: Put yourself in the
customer's place.
Orison Swett Marden

288

Statistics suggest that when customers complain, business owners
and managers ought to get excited about it. The complaining
customer represents a huge opportunity of more business.
Zig Ziglar

289
Today's distracted consumers, bombarded with information and options, often struggle to find the products or services that will best meet their needs.
Harvard Business Review (HBR)

290
Nothing is ever gained by winning an argument and losing a customer.
C.F. Norton

291
Loyal customers, they don't just come back, they don't simply recommend you, they insist that their friends do business with you.
Chip R. Bell

292
Everyone is not your customer.
Seth Godin

293
If you do build a great experience, customers tell each other about that. Word of mouth is very powerful.
Jeff Bezos

294
One customer, well taken care of, could be more valuable than $10,000 worth of advertising.
Jim Rohn

295
Customers remember the service a lot longer than they remember the price.
Lauren Freedman

296
The danger is in acting on what you believe satisfies the customer. You will inevitably make wrong assumptions.
Peter F. Drucker

297
The customer is the most important person in a free market economy. The rule is this: If the customer likes you and trusts you, the details will not get in the way of the sale. If the prospect however, is neutral toward you, or even worse, negative, the details will trip you up every step of the way.
Brian Tracy

298
The golden rule for every businessman is this: Put yourself in your customer's place.
Mark Hunter

299
Talk to unhappy customers.
Linda Sanford

300
I have always believed you cannot run a successful enterprise from behind a desk.
Lou Gerstner

301
Spend a lot of time talking to customers face to face. You'd be amazed how many companies don't listen to their customers.
Ross Perot

302
Your most unhappy customers are your greatest source of learning.
Bill Gates

9. Customer Care

303
Profit is the celebration of service.
Denis Waitley

304
The world is changing and it's time to get customer obsessed.
Sheryl Pattek

305
You'll never have a product or price advantage again. They can be easily duplicated, but a strong customer service culture can't be copied.
Jerry Fritz

306
The best marketing strategy ever: CARE
Gary Vaynerchuk

307
The goal as a company is to have customer service that is not just the best, but legendary.
Sam Walton

308
The 'Ultimate Question' in all customer service and sales activities is 'Would you recommend us to others?'
Fred Reichold

309
Customer service is the new marketing.
Derek Sivers

310
Taking care of your ' customers means more than price, product and delivery. It means showing you care about them. As individual, living, breathing human beings.
Harvey Mackay

311
There are many who subscribe to the convention that service is a business cost, but our data demonstrates that superior service is an investment that can help drive business growth. Investing in quality talent, and ensuring they have the skills, training and tools that enable them to empathize and actively listen to customers are central to providing consistently excellent service experiences.
Jim Bush

312
Simply managing data about customers is no substitute for ensuring that the customers are satisfied with their experience of the company.
Philip Kotler

313
It is not your customer's job to remember you. It is your obligation and responsibility to make sure they don't have the chance to forget you.
Patricia Fripp

314

The issue is not your competition. It's your relationship with the customer and whether or not they feel you have their best interests at heart.
Ron Karr

315

If you don't serve the customer, then your job is to serve someone who does it.
Philip Kotler

316

Customer service is not a department, it's everyone's job.
Ken Blanchard

317

If you are not taking care of your customer, your competitor will.
Bob Hooey

318

Courteous treatment will make a customer a walking advertisement.
James Cash Penny

319

Here is a simple but powerful rule … always give people more than they expect to get.
Nelson Boswell

320

Your customers don't care how much you know until they know how much you care.
Damon Richards

10.   Decisiveness

321
It is in your moments of decision that your destiny is shaped.
Tony Robbins

322
Our lives are a sum total of the choices we have made.
Wayne Dyer

323
Decisiveness is a characteristic of high-performing men and women. Almost any decision is better than no decision at all.
Brian Tracy

324
The best decision is the right decision. The next best decision is the wrong decision. The worst decision is no decision.
Scott McNealy

325
If I had to sum up in one word what makes a good manager, I'd say decisiveness. You can use the fanciest computers to gather the numbers, but in the end you have to set a timetable and act.
Lee Iacocca

326
I am not a product of my circumstances. I am a product of my decisions.
Stephen Covey

327
Every choice you make has an end result.
Zig Ziglar

328
Good judgment comes from experience, and often experience comes from bad judgment.
Rita Mae Brown

329
When I've heard all I need to make a decision, I don't take a vote. I make a decision.
Ronald Reagan

330
Checking the results of a decision against its expectation shows executives what their strengths are, where they need to improve, and where they lack knowledge or information.
Peter F. Drucker

11.   Education & Knowledge

331
Live as if you were to die tomorrow. Learn as if you were to live forever.
Mahatma Gandhi

332
Knowledge has become the key economic resource and the dominant, if not the only, source of competitive advantage.
Peter F. Drucker

333
If you think education is expensive just try ignorance.
Derek Bok

334
If you can't explain it to a six year old, you don't understand it yourself.
Albert Einstein

335
Everything you are learning is preparing you for something else…
Marjorie Pay Hinckley

336
Formal education will make you a living; self-education will make you a fortune.
Jim Rohn

337
If you are not willing to learn, no one can help you. If you are determined to learn, no one can stop you.
Unknown

338
If you want to earn more, learn more.
Zig Ziglar

339
The only true wisdom is in knowing you know nothing.
Socrates

340
I am always doing that which I cannot do, in order that I may learn how to do it.
Pablo Picasso

341
The most important, and indeed the truly unique, contribution of management in the 20th century was the fifty-fold increase in the productivity of the MANUAL WORKER in manufacturing. The most important contribution management needs to make in the 21st century is similarly to increase the productivity of KNOWLEDGE WORK and the KNOWLEDGE WORKER.
Peter F. Drucker

342
I never learn anything by talking. I only learn things when I ask questions.
Lou Holtz

343
Education is progressive discovery of our ignorance.
Will Durant

344
One sure-fire way to stay creative: force yourself to learn
something new.
Harvey Mackay

345
Information is not knowledge.
Albert Einstein

346
I have never in my life learned anything from any man who
agreed with me.
Dudley Field Malone

347
There is no education like adversity.
Benjamin Disraeli

348
Give a man a fish and you feed him for a day; teach a man to fish
and you feed him for a lifetime.
Chinese Proverb

349
Knowledge of men is the prime secret of business success.
Darius Ogden Mills

12.   Failure

350
I have not failed. I've just found 10000 ways that won't work.
Thomas A. Edison

351
I've missed more than 9000 shots in my career. I've lost almost
300 games. Twenty six times I have been trusted to take the
game winning shot and missed. I've failed over and over again in
my life-and that is why I succeed.
Michael Jordan

352
Failure is an event, not a person. Yesterday ended last night.
Today is a brand-new day and it's yours.
Zig Ziglar

353
Doubt has killed more dreams than failure ever will.
Suzy Kassem

354
Every defeat, every heartbreak, every loss, contains its own seed,
its own lesson on how to improve your performance the next
time.
Og Mandino

355
Most great people have attained their greatest success one step beyond their greatest failure.
Napoleon Hill

356
Success is the ability to go from failure to failure without losing your enthusiasm.
Winston Churchill

357
Sometimes you win, sometimes you learn.
John Maxwell

358
It is impossible to live without failing at something, unless you live so cautiously that you might as well not have lived at all - in which case, you fail by default.
J. K. Rowling

359
The master has failed more times than the beginner has even tried.
Stephen McCranie

360
Confidence and hard work are the best medicine to kill the disease called failure. It will make you a successful person.
A.P.J. Abdul Kalam

361

If we learn from losing, we become winners in the end.
Unknown

362

The road to success is paved with disappointment. Losers call it failure; winners call it feedback.
Michael Angier

363

I never see failure as failure, but only as the game I must play and win.
Tom Hopkins

364

We need to accept that we won't always make the right decisions, that we'll screw up royally sometimes - understanding that failure is not the opposite of success, it's part of success.
Arianna Huffington

365

If you try you might fail, but if you don't try you'll never succeed.
Thomas A. Knight

366

Ambitious failure, magnificent failure, is a very good thing.
Guy Kawasaki

367

You don't drown by falling into water. You only drown if you stay there.
Zig Ziglar

368
Failure should be our teacher, not our undertaker. Failure is delay, not defeat. It is a temporary detour, not a dead end.
Denis Waitley

369
Failure is simply an opportunity to begin again, this time more intelligently.
Henry Ford

370
There is a long bridge between I failed and I am a failure. Do not cross that bridge when you come to it!
Unknown

371
It is not a disgrace to fail. Failing is one of the greatest arts in the world.
Charles Kettering

372
Failure is the condiment that gives success its flavor.
Truman Capote

373
It's fine to celebrate success but it's more important to heed the lessons of failure.
Bill Gates

374
Each failure brings you one step closer to success.
Zig Ziglar

375

One of the best predictors of ultimate success ... isn't natural talent or even industry expertise, but how you explain your failures and rejections.

Daniel H. Pink

376

I have learnt more from my failures than my successes.

Richard Branson

377

A failure is a man who has blundered but is not capable of cashing in on the experience.

Elbert Hubbard

13.   Fear

378
Everything you've ever wanted is on the other side of fear.
George Addair

379
Too many of us are not living our dreams because we are living
our fears.
Les Brown

380
We have nothing to fear but fear itself.
Franklin D. Roosevelt

381
Do one thing every day that scares you.
Eleanor Roosevelt

382
If it scares you, it might be a good thing to try.
Seth Godin

383
It is not failure itself that holds you back; it is the fear of failure
that paralyzes you.
Brian Tracy

384
Our greatest fear should not be of failure but of succeeding at things in life that don't really matter.
Francis Chan

385
Do what you fear most and you control fear.
Tom Hopkins

386
Be not afraid of going slowly, be afraid only of standing still.
Chinese Proverb

387
What we fear doing most is usually what we most need to do.
Tim Ferriss

388
Sometimes what you're most afraid of doing is the very thing that will set you free.
Unknown

389
Fear is the destroyer of dreams and the killer of ambitions.
Jeffrey Benjamin

390
You gain strength, courage and confidence by every experience in which you really stop to look fear in the face...You must do the thing you think you cannot do.
Eleanor Roosevelt

391

If you want to conquer fear, don't sit home and think about it.
Go out and get busy.
Dale Carnegie

392

Decide that you want it more than you are afraid of it.
Bill Cosby

393

Do you really want to look back on your life and see how
wonderful it could have been had you not been afraid to live it?
Caroline Myss

394

Think of the times you flowed through fear, did it anyway, and
came out fantastic! This will train your mind that you can do it
again and again... Bigger... Better... Brighter and Bolder!
Kim Somers Egelsee

395

A superior man is one who is free from fear and anxieties.
Confucius

396

When you do the right things in the right way, you have nothing
to lose because you have nothing to fear.
Zig Ziglar

14.   Focus & Priority

397
You can do anything, but not everything.
David Allen

398
Few of us ever live in the present. We are forever anticipating
what is to come or remembering what has gone.
Louis L' Amour

399
Things which matter most must never be at the mercy of things
which matter least.
Johann Wolfgang Goethe

400
Because we don't know what is really important to us, everything
seems important. Because everything seems important, we have
to do everything. Other people, unfortunately, see us as doing
everything, so they expect us to do everything. Doing everything
keeps us so busy, we don't have time to think about what is really
important to us.
Unknown

401
The successful warrior is the average man, with laser-like focus.
Bruce Lee

402
Always remember, your focus determines your reality.
Qui-Gon Jinn

403
Focus on being productive instead of busy.
Tim Ferriss

404
Your success will be largely determined by your ability to concentrate single-mindedly on one thing at a time.
Brian Tracy

405
You always have time for the things you put first.
Unknown

406
Don't mistake movement for achievement. It's easy to get faked out by being busy. The question is: "Busy doing What?"
Jim Rohn

407
Stop managing your time. Start managing your focus.
Robin Sharma

408
It is a mistake to look too far ahead. Only one link of the chain of destiny can be handled at a time.
Winston Churchill

409
The key is not to prioritize what's on your schedule, but to schedule your priorities.
Stephen Covey

410
Stop being afraid of what could go wrong and focus on what could go right.
Unknown

411
What you focus on expands. So focus on what you want, not what you do not want.
Esther Jno-Charles

412
Lack of direction, not lack of time, is the problem. We all have twenty-four hour days.
Zig Ziglar

413
The ability to focus attention on important things is a defining characteristic of intelligence.
Robert J Shiller

15.   Hard Work

414
If you trust in yourself... and believe in your dreams... and follow your star... you'll still get beaten by people who spent their time working hard and learning things and weren't so lazy.
Terry Pratchett

415
Hard work beat talent when talent doesn't work hard.
Tim Notke

416
Luck has nothing to do with it, because I have spent many, many hours, countless hours, on the court working for my one moment in time, not knowing when it would come.
Serena Williams

417
The harder I work, the luckier I get.
Unknown

418
No one limits your growth but you. If you want to earn more, learn more. That means you'll work harder for a while; that means you'll work longer for a while. But you'll be paid for your extra effort with enhanced earnings down the road.
Tom Hopkins

419
There is no substitute for hard work.
Thomas A. Edison

420
You will succeed because most people are lazy.
Unknown

421
Hard work has made it easy. That is my secret. That is why I
win.
Nadia Comaneci

422
If you can't outplay them, outwork them.
Ben Hogan

423
To be really successful in your career, you have to start a little
earlier, you have to work a little harder, and you have to stay a
little later.
Brian Tracy

424
Opportunities are usually disguised as hard work, so most people
don't recognize them.
Ann Landers

425
If people knew how hard I worked to achieve my mastery, it
wouldn't seem so wonderful after all.
Michelangelo

426
Don't be like most salespeople who are unwilling to do the hard
work it takes to make selling easy.
Jeffrey Gitomer

427
Good ideas are common - what's uncommon are
people who'll work hard enough to bring them about.
Ashleigh Brilliant

428
Plans are only good intentions unless they immediately
degenerate into hard work.
Peter F. Drucker

429
Entrepreneurship is living few years of your life like most people
won't, so that you can spend the rest of your life like most people
can't.
Unknown

16.　Inspirational

430
Thought about quitting. Then I noticed who was watching.
Unknown

431
The creation of a thousand forests is in one acorn.
Ralph Waldo Emerson

432
Don't you dare give up!
Yvonne Jeanee-Theresa Person

433
I want to inspire people. I want someone to look at me and say
"because of you I didn't give up."
Unknown

434
The difference between what we are doing and what we are
capable of doing would solve world's most problem.
Mahatma Gandhi

435
Life is not measured by the number of breaths we take, but by
the moments that take our breath away.
Vicki Corona

436

Let others lead small lives, but not you. Let others argue over small things, but not you. Let others cry over small hurts, but not you. Let others leave their future in someone else's hands, but not you.
Jim Rohn

437

Never give up on something that you can't go a day without thinking about.
Winston Churchill

438

That which doesn't kill us makes us stronger.
Friedrich Nietzsche

439

Your time is limited, so don't waste it living someone else's life. Don't be trapped by dogma - which is living with the results of other people's thinking. Don't let the noise of others' opinions drown out your own inner voice. And most important, have the courage to follow your heart and intuition. They somehow already know what you truly want to become. Everything else is secondary.
Steve Jobs

440

It is our darkest moments that we must focus to see the light.
Aristotle Onassis

441

When I stand before God at the end of my life, I would hope that I would not have a single bit of talent left, and could say, "I used everything you gave me."
Erma Bombeck

442

Rock bottom became the solid foundation on which I rebuilt my life.
J. K. Rowling

443

My sun sets to rise again?
Elizabeth Barrett Browning

444

The soul would rather fail at its own life than succeed at someone else's.
David Whyte

445

You may encounter many defeats but we must not be defeated.
Maya Angelou

446

Don't quit. Suffer now and live the rest of your life as a champion.
Muhammad Ali

447

Don't cry because it's over, smile because it happened.
Theodor Seuss Geisel (Dr. Seuss)

448
Success is making those who believed in you look brilliant.
Dharmesh Shah

449
You are GOOD enough, SMART enough, BEAUTIFUL
enough, and STRONG enough. Believe it and never let
insecurity run your life.
Unknown

450
The only thing you ever have is now.
Eckhart Tolle

451
The power of imagination makes us infinite.
John Muir

452
All I need is a sheet of paper and something to write with, and
then I can turn the world upside down.
Friedrich Nietzsche

453
If your WHY is strong enough you will figure out the HOW!
Bill Walsh

454
When you've exhausted all your possibilities, remember this - you
haven't.
Thomas A. Edison

455
Nothing is as powerful as an idea whose time has come.
Victor Hugo

456
How can you squander even one more day not taking advantage of the greatest shifts of our generation? How dare you settle for less when the world had made it so easy for you to be remarkable?
Seth Godin

457
You may write me down in history With your bitter, twisted lies, You may trod me in the very dirt But still, like dust, I'll rise.
Maya Angelou

458
Our deepest fear is not that we are inadequate. Our deepest fear is that we are powerful beyond measure. It is our light, not our darkness, that most frightens us. Your playing small does not serve the world. There is nothing enlightened about shrinking so that other people won't feel insecure around you. We are all meant to shine as children do. It's not just in some of us; it is in everyone. And as we let our own lights shine, we unconsciously give other people permission to do the same. As we are liberated from our own fear, our presence automatically liberates others.
Marianne Williamson

459
Someone is sitting in the shade today because someone planted a tree a long time ago.
Warren Buffett

460
Put your heart, mind, and soul into even your smallest acts. This is the secret of success.
Swami Sivananda

461
I don't know what your destiny will be, but one thing I know: the only ones among you who will be really happy are those who will have sought and found how to serve.
Albert Schweitzer

462
Don't judge each day by the harvest you reap but by the seeds that you plant.
Robert Louis Stevenson

463
If you work just for money, you'll never make it. But if you love what you are doing, and always put the customer first, success will be yours.
Ray Kroc

464
Help one another; there's no time like the present and no present like time.
James Durst

465
Nothing is impossible, the word itself says 'I'm possible!'
Audrey Hepburn

466
My life is my message.
Mahatma Gandhi

467
Yesterday is gone. Tomorrow has not yet come. We have only
today. Let us begin.
Mother Teresa

468
Champions aren't made in gyms. Champions are made from
something they have deep inside them - a desire, a dream, a
vision. They have to have the skill, and the will. But the will
must be stronger than the skill.
Muhammad Ali

469
Two roads diverged in a wood and I - I took the one less traveled
by, and that has made all the difference.
Robert Frost

470
You are here for a reason.
Unknown

471
The best revenge is massive success.
Frank Sinatra

472
I am the master of my fate, I am the captain of my soul.
William Ernest Henley

473

So many of our dreams at first seem impossible, then they seem
improbable, and then, when we summon the will, they soon
become inevitable.
Christopher Reeve

474

It's kind of fun to do the impossible.
Walt Disney

475

Until you are broken, you don't know what you're made of. Being
broken gives you the ability to build yourself all over again, but
this time around build yourself stronger than ever. Therefore you
will be unbreakable.
Melissa Molomo

476

To every man there comes in his lifetime that special moment;
that moment, when he is figuratively tapped on the shoulder and
offered a chance to do a very special thing, unique to him and
fitted for his talents. What a tragedy,
if that moment finds him unprepared, or unqualified, for the
work which would be his finest hour.
Winston Churchill

477

You must be the change you wish to see in the world.
Mahatma Gandhi

478
Even the greatest was once a beginner. Don't be afraid to take that first step.
Muhammad Ali

479
You have within you right now, everything you need to deal with whatever the world can throw at you.
Brian Tracy

480
It's time that you realise you're worth a hell of a lot more than you think.
Unknown

481
To be truly happy, you need a clear sense of meaning and purpose in life.
Brian Tracy

482
There are no limits on what you can achieve with your life, except the limits you accept in your mind.
Brian Tracy

483
There's no need to be perfect to inspire others. Let people get inspired by how you deal with your imperfections.
Robert Tew

484

Enthusiasm is the mother of effort; and without it nothing great was ever accomplished.
Ralph Waldo Emerson

485

You can do anything if you have enthusiasm. Enthusiasm is the yeast that makes your hopes rise to the stars. Enthusiasm is the sparkle in your eyes, the swing in your gait, the grip of your hand, the irresistible surge of will and energy to execute your ideas. Enthusiasts are fighters. They have fortitude. They have staying qualities. Enthusiasm is at the bottom of all progress. With it, there is accomplishment. Without it, there are only alibis.
Henry Ford

486

Try to be a rainbow in someone's cloud.
Maya Angelou

487

Let each of us aspire to inspire, before we expire.
Eugene Bell Jr.

488

It doesn't matter where you are coming from. All that matters is where you are going.
Brian Tracy

489

Make today count. You'll never get it back.
Unknown

490
Always keep your eyes open. Keep watching. Because whatever you see can inspire you.
Grace Coddington

491
I got lucky because I never gave up the search. Are you quitting too soon? Or are you willing to pursue luck with a vengeance?
Jill Konrath

492
I know why I am here and my only real focused goal is to live each day to the fullest and to try and honor God and be an encouragement to others. What the future holds is firmly in God's hands, and I am very happy about that!"
Ken Hensley

493
Write your future.
Unknown

494
All our dreams can come true if we have the courage to pursue them.
Walt Disney

495
I may win and I may lose but I will never be defeated.
Emmitt Smith

496
Rock bottom has built way more champions than privilege.

Unknown

497
It's not whether you get knocked down, it's whether you get up.
Vince Lombardi

498
Your wings already exist. All you have to do is fly.
Unknown

499
Winners never quit and quitters never win.
Vince Lombardi

500
No one is going to hand me success. I must go out & get it
myself. That's why I'm here. To dominate. To conquer. Both the
world, and myself.
Unknown

501
Believe and act as if it were impossible to fail.
Charles Kettering

502
You gotta be hungry!
Les Brown

503
There is no exercise better for the heart than reaching down and
lifting people up.
John Holmes

504

If you always put limit on everything you do, physical or anything else. It will spread into your work and into your life. There are no limits. There are only plateaus, and you must not stay there, you must go beyond them.
Bruce Lee

505

The superior man is the providence of the inferior. He is eyes for the blind, strength for the weak, and a shield for the defenseless. He stands erect by bending above the fallen. He rises by lifting others.
Robert Ingersoll

506

Ideas are the beginning points of all fortunes.
Napoleon Hill

507

Failure will never overtake me if my determination to succeed is strong enough.
Og Mandino

508

Worry is a misuse of your imagination.
Dan Zadra

509

There is no ceiling in effort.
Harvey C. Fruehauf

510
You only have to succeed the last time.
Brian Tracy

511
He who cannot change the very fabric of his thought will never be able to change reality, and will never, therefore, make any progress.
Anwar Sadat

512
Memories of our lives, of our works and our deeds will continue in others.
Rosa Parks

513
Act with purpose, courage, confidence, competence and intelligence until these qualities "lock in" to your subconscious mind.
Brian Tracy

514
You can't win unless you first begin. So start now.
Robin Sharma

515
It's a terrible thing, I think, in life to wait until you're ready. I have this feeling now that actually no one is ever ready to do anything. There is almost no such thing as ready. There is only now. And you may as well do it now. Generally speaking, now is as good a time as any.
Hugh Laurie

516
I believe in living today. Not in yesterday, nor in tomorrow.
Loretta Young

517
Do something today that your future self will thank you for.
Unknown

518
I know of no more encouraging fact than the unquestionable ability of man to elevate his life by conscious endeavor.
Henry David Thoreau

519
The best way to predict the future is to create it.
Alan Kay

520
You are a potential genius; there is no problem you cannot solve, and no answer you cannot find somewhere.
Brian Tracy

521
Light tomorrow with today.
Elizabeth Barrett Browning

522
I've learned that people will forget what you said, people will forget what you did, but people will never forget how you made them feel.
Maya Angelou

523
She took the leap and built her wings on the way down.
Kobi Yamada

524
You can't use up creativity. The more you use, the more you have.
Maya Angelou

525
Your imagination is ten times more potent than your willpower. Unleashed, it provides a sense of certainty and tenacious vision that goes far beyond any limitation of the past.
Tony Robbins

526
May the space between where I am and where I want to be inspire me.
Tracee Ellis Ross

527
It always seems impossible until it's done.
Nelson Mandela

528
Never say the sky is the limit when there are footprints on the moon!
Paul Brandt

529
Learn to live on the edge.
Richard Branson

530
Every moment is a fresh beginning.
T. S. Eliot

531
Imagination is more important than knowledge.
Albert Einstein

532
You will enjoy any activity in which you are fully present...
Eckhart Tolle

533
Beginning today, treat everyone you meet as if they were going to be dead by midnight. Extend to them all the care, kindness and understanding you can muster, and do it with no thought of any reward. Your life will never be the same again.
Og Mandino

17.   Leadership

534
Leaders don't create followers. They create more leaders.
Tom Peters

535
With great power comes great responsibility.
Voltaire

536
If anything goes bad, I did it. If anything goes semi-good, we did it. If anything goes really good, then you did it. That's all it takes to get people to win football games for you.
Paul Bryant

537
The art of leadership is saying no, not saying yes. It is very easy to say yes.
Tony Blair

538
The golden rule of leadership, and life. Do the right thing all of the time.
Jeffrey Gitomer

539
Leadership is about making others better as a result of your presence and making sure that impact lasts in your absence.
Sheryl Sandberg

540
Failing organizations are usually over-managed and under-led.
Warren Bennis

541
A leader takes people where they want to go. A great leader takes people where they don't necessarily want to go, but ought to be.
Rosalynn Carter

542
Management is doing things right; leadership is doing the right things.
Peter F. Drucker

543
Leadership is solving problems. The day soldiers stop bringing you their problems is the day you have stopped leading them. They have either lost confidence that you can help or concluded you do not care. Either case is a failure of leadership.
Colin Powell

544
Be the kind of leader that you would follow. Be the type of person you want to meet. Be who you needed when you were younger.
Unknown

545
Be the ambassador for what you stand for.
Nisha Moodley

546

No person can be a great leader unless he takes genuine joy in the successes of those under him.
W. A. Nance

547

If you want to lead the orchestra, you must turn your back on the crowd.
Max Lucado

548

The best minute I spend is the one I invest in people.
Kenneth H. Blanchard

549

Be a voice, not an echo.
Albert Einstein

550

Treat a man as he is, and he will remain as he is. Treat a man as he could be, and he will become what he should be.
Ralph Waldo Emerson

551

As we look into the next century, leaders will be those who empower others.
Bill Gates

552

Accountability breeds response-ability.
Stephen Covey

553
Leaders have to search for the heart on a team, because the person who has it can bring out the best in everybody else.
Mike Krzyzewski

554
Few things can help an individual more than to place responsibility on him, and to let him know that you trust him.
Booker T. Washington

18. Life

555
Sometimes I wish I could go back in life. Not to change things, just to feel a couple things twice.
Drake

556
We do not remember days, we remember moments.
Cesare Pavese

557
The way a person does one thing is the way they do everything.
Unknown

558
What we are is God's gift to us. What we become is our gift to God.
Eleanor Powell

559
Twenty years from now you will be more disappointed by the things that you didn't do than by the ones you did do. So throw off the bowlines. Sail away from the safe harbor. Catch the trade winds in your sails. Explore. Dream. Discover.
H. Jackson Brown, Jr.

560
No other success can compensate for failure in the home.
David McKay

561
Wisdom is an equal measure of experience plus reflection.
Aristotle, Greek Philosopher

562
The people you love, and who love you, are the real measure of
how well you are doing as a human being.
Brian Tracy

563
Don't live the same year 75 times and call it a life.
Robin Sharma

564
Circumstances don't make the man, they only reveal him to
himself.
Epictetus

565
It takes time to build a corporate work of art. It takes time to
build a life. And it takes time to develop and grow. So give
yourself, your enterprise, and your family the time they deserve
and the time they require.
Jim Rohn

566
Life begins at the end of your comfort zone.
Neale Donald Walsch

567
The best and most beautiful things in the world cannot be seen
or even touched - they must be felt with the heart.
Helen Keller

568
It's your place in the world; it's your life. Go on and do all you
can with it, and make it the life you want to live.
Mae Jemison

569
Sometimes when I consider what tremendous consequences
come from little things. I am tempted to think there are no little
things.
Bruce Barton

570
Never make permanent decisions on temporary feelings.
Wiz Khalifa

571
You've gotta dance like there's nobody watching,
Love like you'll never be hurt,
Sing like there's nobody listening,
And live like it's heaven on earth.
William W. Purkey

572
You only live once, but if you do it right, once is enough.
Mae West

573
The unexamined life is not worth living.
Socrates

574
To go faster, you must slow down.
John Brunner

575
Ability is what you're capable of doing. Motivation determines what you do. Attitude determines how well you do it.
Lee Holz

576
There is no real excellence in all this world which can be separated from right living.
David Starr Jordan

577
If you want to go fast, go alone. If you want to go far, go with others.
African Proverb

578
If you find yourself in a hole the first thing to do is stop digging.
Will Rogers

579
Work hard, stay humble, be kind.
Unknown

580

Without gratitude and appreciation for what you already have,
you'll never know true fulfillment.
Tony Robbins

581

The quality of your life is determined by the quality of your
relationships. The quality of your business is no different.
Harvey Mackay

582

In the end, life lived to its fullest is its own Ultimate Gift.
Jim Stovall

583

The heart has its reasons which reason knows not of.
Blaise Pascal

584

Manage Your Energy, Not Your Time.
Tony Schwartz

585

We have committed the Golden Rule to memory; let us now
commit it to life.
Edwin Markham

586

Be happy with what you have while working for what you want.
Helen Keller

587
Laughter is timeless, imagination has no age, dreams are forever.
Walt Disney

588
There are skills we can take wherever we go in life, no matter what we do.
Millie Hogue

589
Life is too short to worry about stupid things. Have fun. Fall in love. Regret nothing, and don't let people bring you down.
Unknown

590
It is a good thing to be rich and a good thing to be strong, but it is a better thing to be loved by many friends.
Euripides

591
Simplification is one of the most difficult things to do.
Jonathan Ive

592
Great minds discuss concepts, Average minds discuss events, Small minds discuss others, Minute minds only discuss themselves.
Eleanor Roosevelt

593
At the end of the day, let there be no excuses, no explanations, no regrets.
Steve Maraboli

594

The best thing to give to your enemy is forgiveness; to an opponent, tolerance; to a friend, your heart; to your child, a good example; to a father, deference; to your mother, conduct that will make her proud of you; to yourself, respect; to all others, charity.
Benjamin Franklin

595

Whenever you find yourself on the side of the majority, it is time to pause and reflect.
Mark Twain

596

The price of anything is the amount of life you exchange for it.
Henry David Thoreau

597

Life is the most difficult exam. Many people fail because they try to copy others. Not realizing that everyone has a different question paper.
Unknown

598

You control just three things: Your actions, your reactions, and your attitude.
Jeb Blount

599

From what we get, we can make a living; what we give, however, makes a life.
Arthur Ashe

600
If you want to feel rich, just count the things you
have that money can't buy.
Unknown

601
With people, if you want to save time, don't be efficient. Slow is
fast and fast is slow.
Stephen Covey

602
You cannot have a positive life and a negative mind.
Joyce Meyer

603
So many people tiptoe through life, so carefully, to arrive, safely,
at death.
Tony Campolo

604
Life is like riding a bicycle. To keep your balance, you must keep
moving.
Albert Einstein

605
A moment of patience in a moment of anger saves you a hundred
moments of regret.
Unknown

606
The definition of insanity is doing the same thing over and over
again, but expecting different results.
Albert Einstein

607
The most important thing is to enjoy your life - to be happy - it's all that matters.
Audrey Hepburn

608
He had had a lot of trouble in his life but most of it never happened.
Mark Twain

609
If you cannot control your emotions, you cannot control your money.
Warren Buffett

610
Life is nothing but a mirror of your consistent thoughts.
Tony Robbins

611
Those who cannot remember the past are condemned to repeat it.
George Santayana

19.   Listening

612
The most important thing in communication is to hear what isn't being said.
Peter F. Drucker

613
God gave us mouths that close and ears that don't, that must tell us something.
Eugene O'Neill

614
Most people do not listen with the intent to understand; they listen with the intent to reply.
Stephen Covey

615
Speak is such a way that others love to listen to you. Listen in such a way that others love to speak to you.
Unknown

616
By far the best way to influence people is to start by really listening to them.
Charles H. Green

617

You can win more friends with your ears than with your mouth.
People who feel like they're being listened to feel accepted and
appreciated. They feel like they're being taken seriously and what
they say really matters.
Harvey Mackay

618

A good listener is not only popular everywhere, but after a while
he knows something.
Wilson Mizner

619

Knowledge talks. Wisdom listens.
Jimi Hendrix

20. Motivational

620

You must not only aim right, but draw the bow with all your might.
Henry David Thoreau

621

No matter what you're going through, there's a light at the end of the tunnel and it may seem hard to get to it but you can do it and just keep working towards it and you'll find the positive side of things.
Demi Lovato

622

When you want to succeed as much as you want to breathe, that's when you will be successful.
Eric Thomas

623

I am here for a purpose and that purpose is to grow into a mountain, not shrink to a grain of sand. Henceforth will I apply all my efforts to become the highest mountain of all and I will strain my potential until it cries for mercy.
Og Mandino

624

If the sun comes up, I have a chance.
Venus Williams

625

The clock is running. Make the most of today. Time waits for no man. Yesterday is history. Tomorrow is a mystery. Today is a gift. That's why it is called the present.
Alice Morse Earle

626

If we have our own 'why' of life, we can bear almost any 'how.'
Friedrich Nietzsche

627

If you saw the size of the blessing coming, you would understand the magnitude of the battle you are fighting.
Joyce Meyer

628

Tough times never last, but tough people do.
Robert H. Schuller

629

Don't wish it were easier, wish you were better.
Jim Rohn

630

I'm not telling you it is going to be easy, I'm telling you it's going to be worth it.
Art Williams

631
Being the richest man in the cemetery doesn't matter to me.
Going to bed at night saying we've done something wonderful,
that's what matters to me.
Steve Jobs

632
Hope is not a strategy. Luck is not a factor. Fear is not an option.
James Cameron

633
At least three times every day take a moment and ask yourself
what is really important. Have the wisdom and the courage to
build your life around your answer.
Lee Jampolsky

634
The phoenix must burn to emerge.
Janet Fitch

635
If you want to test your memory, try to recall what you were
worrying about one year ago today.
E. Joseph Cossman

636
If you aren't going all the way, why go at all?
Joe Namath

637
When something bad happens you have three choices. You can either let it define you. Let it destroy you, or you can let it strengthen you.
Theodor Seuss Geisel (Dr. Seuss)

638
Be strong when you are weak, brave when you are scared and humble when you are victorious.
Unknown

639
There is only one way to avoid criticism: do nothing, say nothing, and be nothing.
Elbert Hubbard

640
When you think you can't - revisit a previous triumph.
Jack Canfield

641
Make each day your masterpiece.
John Wooden

642
If you have everything under control, you're not moving fast enough.
Mario Andretti

643
There is no greater agony than bearing an untold story inside you.
Maya Angelou

644
'Finished last' will always be better than 'did not finish', which always trumps 'did not start.'
Unknown

645
Life is 10% what happens to you and 90% how you react to it.
Charles R Swindoll

646
There are no accidents... there is only some purpose that we haven't yet understood.
Deepak Chopra

647
What a wonderful thought it is that some of the best days of our lives haven't happened yet.
Anne Frank

648
Anything worth having is worth going for - all the way.
J.R. Ewing

649
If you have always done it that way, it is probably wrong.
Charles Kettering

650
Whether you think you can or think you can't, you're right.
Henry Ford

651
Never let success get to your head. Never let failure get to your heart.
Unknown

652
A comfort zone is a beautiful place, but nothing ever grows there. Amazing things rarely happen in your comfort zone.
Unknown

653
Good, better, best. Never let it rest. 'Til your good is better and your better is best.
St Jerome

654
Every day may not be good... but there's something good in every day.
Alice Morse Earle

655
Do not pray for easy lives. Pray to be stronger men! Do not pray for tasks equal to your powers. Pray for powers equal to your tasks!
Phillips Brooks

656
Good is the enemy of great.
Jim Collins

657
The most unprofitable item ever manufactured is an excuse.
John Mason

658
Don't stop when you're tired. Stop when you're done.
Unknown

659
Every morning you have two choices, continue your sleep with dreams or wake up and chase your dreams. Choice is yours.
Unknown

660
It's not the size of the dog in the fight, but the size of the fight in the dog.
Archie Griffin

661
Mile by mile it's a trial; yard by yard it's hard; but inch by inch it's a cinch.
Unknown

662
If you don't design your own life plan, chances are you'll fall into someone else's plan. And guess what they have planned for you? Not much.
Jim Rohn

663
How do you deal with rejection? Pretend they say, "It's not you. It's me." Because that is essentially what they mean.
Emma Walton Hamilton

664
If you cannot do great things, do small things in a great way.
Napoleon Hill

665
We are what we repeatedly do. Excellence then is not an act but
a habit.
Will Durant

666
You can't let your past hold your future hostage.
LL Cool J

667
You can't let praise or criticism get to you. It's a weakness to get
caught up in either one.
John Wooden

668
Always make a total effort, even when the odds are against you.
Arnold Palmer

669
Be miserable. Or motivate yourself. Whatever has to be done, it's
always your choice.
Wayne Dyer

670
Don't be distracted by criticism. Remember the only taste of
success some people have is when they take a bite out of you.
Zig Ziglar

671
Ever tired. Ever failed. No matter. Try again. Fail again. Fail better.
Samuel Beckett

672
He who worries about calamities suffers them twice over.
Og Mandino

673
The difference between MUST & SHOULD is the life you want and the life you have.
Tony Robbins

674
I'm not where I need to be, but thank God I'm not where I used to be.
Joyce Meyer

675
Every morning brings new potential, but if you dwell on the misfortunes of the day before, you tend to overlook tremendous opportunities.
Harvey Mackay

676
Perfection is not attainable, but if we chase perfection we can catch excellence.
Vince Lombardi

677
One finds limits by pushing them.
Herbert Simon

678
We sometimes feel that what we do is just a drop in the ocean, but the ocean would be less because of that missing drop.
Mother Teresa

679
You will never reach your destination if you stop and throw stones at every dog that barks.
Winston Churchill

680
It's not can you, it's will you.
Tony Robbins

681
If it matters to you, who cares if it matters to anyone else.
Unknown

682
Don't count the days, make the days count.
Muhammad Ali

683
There's a difference between giving up and starting over.
Unknown

684
Little minds are tamed and subdued by misfortune; but great minds rise above them.
Washington Irving

685
Don't ruin a good today by thinking about a bad yesterday. Let it go.
Unknown

686
Never mind what others do; do better than yourself, beat your own record from day to day, and you are a success.
William J.H. Boetcker

687
There are no great men. Just great challenges which ordinary men, out of necessity, are forced by circumstance to meet.
William Frederick Halsey Jr.

688
The way you position yourself at the beginning of a relationship has profound impact on where you end up.
Ron Karr

689
Motivation will almost always beat mere talent.
Norman Ralph Augustine

690
If you have enough reasons you can do the most incredible things.
Jim Rohn

691
Motivation is what gets you started. Habit is what keeps you going.
Jim Rohn

692
Determination is the wake-up call to the human will.
Tony Robbins

693
Human beings have the remarkable ability to turn nothing into something. They can turn weeds into gardens and pennies into fortunes.
Jim Rohn

694
Thought is the original source of all wealth, all success, all material gain, all great discoveries and inventions, and of all achievement.
Claude Bristol

695
Don't worry about failures, worry about the chances you miss when you don't even try.
Jack Canfield

696
You can't go back and make a new start, but you can start right now and make a brand new ending.
James R. Sherman

697
Develop skills and tool sets that make you better than the best and faster than the rest.
Gerhard Gschwandtner

698
Life's battles don't always go to the strongest or fastest; sooner or later those who win are those who think they can.
Richard Bach

699
We need to forget what we think we are, so that we can really become what we are.
Paulo Coelho

700
You can only see in others what is inside of you.
Zig Ziglar

701
Don't expect a great day; create one.
Bob Proctor

702
Master your strengths, outsource your weaknesses.
Ryan Kahn

703
Three things you cannot recover in life:
1) The MOMENT after it's missed 2) The WORD after it's said, AND 3) The TIME after it's wasted.
Unknown

704
Luck is what happens when preparation meets opportunity.
Seneca

705

There is no genius who hasn't a touch of insanity.
Aristotle, Greek Philosopher

706

The positive thinker sees the invisible, feels the intangible and achieves the impossible.
Winston Churchill

707

The measure of who we are is what we do with what we have.
Vince Lombardi

708

People often say that motivation doesn't last. Well, neither does bathing. That's why we recommend it daily.
Zig Ziglar

709

Don't judge me by my past. I don't live there anymore.
Zig Ziglar

710

When you judge another, you do not define them, you define yourself.
Wayne Walter Dyer

711

Motivation alone is not enough. If you have an idiot and you motivate him, now you have a motivated idiot.
Jim Rohn

712
Become the person who would attract the results you seek.
Jim Cathcart

713
We find comfort among those who agree with
us - growth among those who don't.
Frank A. Clark

714
Don't be upset when people reject you. Nice things are rejected
all the time by people who can't afford them.
Unknown

715
Change your thoughts and you change your world.
Norman Vincent Peale

716
Break through the bonds of your past.
Tony Robbins

717
Your greatest asset is your earning ability. Your greatest resource
is your time.
Brian Tracy

718
The most important thing in life is to stop saying `I wish' and
start saying `I will'. Consider nothing impossible, then treat
possibilities as probabilities.
Charles Dickens

719
Don't limit investing to the financial world. Invest something of yourself, and you will be richly rewarded.
Charles Schwab

720
There are two primary choices in life: to accept conditions as they exist, or accept the responsibility for changing them.
Denis Waitley

721
When you believe something can be done, really believe, your mind will find ways to do it.
David Schwartz

722
Hope for the best, be prepared for the worse. Life is shocking, but you must never appear to be shocked. For no matter how bad it is it could be worse and no matter how good it is it could be better.
Maya Angelou

723
Resilience is not what happens to you. It's how you react to, respond to, and recover from what happens to you.
Jeffrey Gitomer

724
If you just communicate, you can get by, but if you communicate skillfully you can work miracles.
Jim Rohn

725
I am too positive to be doubtful, too optimistic to be fearful, and too determined to be defeated.
Unknown

726
Do what is right. Not what is easy.
Unknown

727
There are two different sides to every Gemini: the happy/relaxed/playful side and the dark/depressed/lazy side.
Unknown

728
Business opportunities are like buses, there's always another one coming.
Richard Branson

729
You begin by always expecting good things to happen.
Tom Hopkins

730
Just one small positive thought in the morning can change your whole day.
Dalai Lama

731
What you feed your mind determines your appetite.
Tom Ziglar

732
Do not let what you cannot do interfere with what you can do.
John Wooden

733
To be outstanding, get comfortable with being uncomfortable.
Alrik Koudenburg

734
You don't get paid for the hour. You get paid for the value you bring to the hour.
Jim Rohn

735
If you want to be rich, don't allow yourself the luxury of excuses.
Robert Kiyosaki

736
It is our choices . . . that show what we truly are, far more than our abilities.
J. K. Rowling

737
Even if you're on the right track, you'll get run over if you just sit there.
Will Rogers

738
Today is always the most productive day of your week.
Mark Hunter

739
Worrying is stupid. It's like walking around with an umbrella
waiting for it to rain.
Wiz Khalifa

740
Only I can change my life. No one else can do it for me.
Carol Burnett

741
There is always room at the top.
Daniel Webster

742
Gratitude unlocks the fullness of life. It turns what we have into
enough, and more. It turns denial into acceptance, chaos to
order, confusion to clarity. It can turn a meal into a feast, a house
into a home, a stranger into a friend.
Melody Beattie

743
Everything you have in your life you have attracted to yourself
because of the person you are.
Brian Tracy

744
I am prepared for the worst, but hope for the best.
Benjamin Disraeli

745
Victory is sweetest when you've known defeat.
Malcolm Forbes

746

He who every morning plans the transactions of the day and follows that plan carries a thread that will guide him through the labyrinth of the most busy life.
Victor Hugo

747

When one door closes another door opens, but we so often look so long and so regretfully upon the closed door, that we do not see the ones which open for us.
Alexander Graham Bell

748

If you don't make a total commitment to whatever you're doing, then start to bail out the first time the boat starts leaking.
Lou Holtz

749

Always bear in mind that your own resolution to succeed is more important than any one thing.
Abraham Lincoln

750

The spirit, the will to win, and the will to excel are the things that endure. These qualities are so much more important than the events that occur.
Vince Lombardi

751

Anything's possible if you've got enough nerve.
J. K. Rowling

752
Motivation is a fire from within. If someone else tries to light that fire under you, chances are it will burn very briefly.
Stephen Covey

753
When everything seems to be going against you, remember that the airplane takes off against the wind, not with it.
Henry Ford

754
What comes easy won't last, what lasts won't come easy.
Unknown

755
You were born to win, but to be a winner, you must plan to win, prepare to win and expect to win.
Zig Ziglar

756
The one thing over which you have complete control is your thinking. Use it well.
Brian Tracy

757
You can never rise higher than your expectations of yourself. Expect the best!
Brian Tracy

758
Faith and fear both demand you believe in something you cannot see. You choose.
Bob Proctor

759

I have found that the more I get my ego out of a picture and the more I think about how can I serve other people instead of always thinking about me, the more miracles show up.
Wayne Dyer

760

Opportunities don't happen, you create them.
Chris Grosser

761

The people who get on in this world are the people who get up and look for the circumstances they want, and if they can't find them, make them.
George Bernard Shaw

762

Almost every successful person begins with two beliefs; the future can be better than the present, and I have the power to make it so.
David Brooks

763

Defeat is not bitter unless you swallow it.
Joe Clark

764

It is never too late to be what you might have been.
George Eliot

765
Do a little more each day than you think you possible can.
Lowell Thomas

766
When you do more than you're paid for, eventually you'll be paid for more than you do.
Zig Ziglar

767
Your only limitations are those you set up in your mind, or permit others to set up for you.
Og Mandino

768
I don't believe you have to be better than everybody else. I believe you have to be better than you ever thought you could be.
Ken Venturi

769
You have to fight through some bad days to earn the best days of your life.
Unknown

770
You must decide exactly what it is you want in life; no one can do this for you.
Brian Tracy

771
Don't be afraid to give up the good to go for the great.
John D. Rockefeller

772
Do what you love, love what you do, and deliver more than you promise.
Harvey Mackay

773
Everyone should have a sense of urgency - it is getting a lot done in a short period of time in a calm and confident manner.
Bob Proctor

774
Your life only gets better when you get better.
Brian Tracy

775
Limitations live only in our minds. But if we use our imaginations, our possibilities become limitless.
Jamie Paolinetti

776
The only person you are destined to become is the person you decide to be.
Ralph Waldo Emerson

777
All of us do not have equal talent. But, all of us have an equal opportunity to develop our talents.
John F. Kennedy

778
Expect the best. Prepare for the worst. Capitalize on what comes.
Zig Ziglar

779
Never let the things you want make you forget the things you have.
Unknown

780
How wonderful it is that nobody need wait a single moment before starting to improve the world.
Anne Frank

781
What lies behind us and what lies before us are tiny matters compared to what lies within us.
Henry Stanley Haskins

782
Opportunity rarely knocks on your door. Knock rather on opportunity's door if you ardently wish to enter.
B. C. Forbes

783
If you're not scaring your boss, you aren't trying hard enough.
Tim Frank

784
High achievement always takes place in the framework of high expectation.
Charles Kettering

785
Find three hobbies you love: one to make you money, one to keep you in shape, and one to be creative.
Unknown

786

What is the driving force propelling every human being forward
in life? Hope.
Unknown

787

Possibilities do not merely add up; they multiply.
Paul Romer

788

The wise man puts himself last and finds himself first.
Lao Tzu

789

Today the greatest single source of wealth is between your ears.
Brian Tracy

790

The man who will use his skill and constructive imagination to
see how much he can GIVE for a dollar, instead of how
LITTLE he can give for a dollar is bound to succeed.
Henry Ford

791

There are only two options: Make progress or make excuses.
Tony Robbins

792

We will receive not what we idly wish for but what we justly
earn. Our rewards will always be in exact proportion to our
service.
Earl Nightingale

793
Look closely at the present you are constructing. It should look like future you are dreaming.
Alice Walker

794
You will get all you want in life if you help enough other people get what they want.
Zig Ziglar

795
Forget about the business outlook, be on the outlook for business.
Paul J. Meyer

21.   Passion

796
Your true passion should feel like breathing; it's that natural.
Oprah Winfrey

797
We all know fear. But passion makes us fearless.
Paulo Coelho

798
If you love what you do, your passion will lead you to success,
and your success will lead to your fulfillment.
Jeffrey Gitomer

799
The people who do the most extraordinary things in the world
are never "realistic." They're passionate. They trust themselves.
Deepak Chopra

800
Passion changes everything.
Ken Robinson

801
If you can't figure out your purpose, figure out your passion. For
your passion will lead you right into your purpose.
T.D. Jakes

802
Find something you're passionate about and keep tremendously
interested in it.
Julia Child

803
Passion without commitment and hard work is like a cart
without a horse - it's not going anywhere.
Mark Sanborn

804
The things you are passionate about are not random, they are
your calling.
Fabienne Fredrickson

805
To succeed you have to believe in something with such a passion
that it becomes a reality.
Anita Roddick

806
We are told that talent creates its own opportunities. But it
sometimes seems that intense desire creates not only its own
opportunities, but its own talents.
Eric Hoffer

22.　Persistence

807

Nothing in this world can take the place of persistence.
Talent will not; nothing is more common than unsuccessful
people with talent.
Genius will not; unrewarded genius is almost a proverb.
Education will not; the world is full of educated derelicts.
Persistence and determination alone are omnipotent.
The slogan "press on" has solved and always will solve the
problems of the human race.
Calvin Coolidge

808

I do not think there is any other quality so essential to success of
any kind as the quality of perseverance. It overcomes almost
everything, even nature.
John D. Rockefeller

809

So long as there is breath in me, that long I will persist. For now
I know one of the greatest principles on success; if I persist long
enough I will win.
Og Mandino

810

Your persistence is a true measure of your belief in yourself and
your ability to succeed.
Brian Tracy

811

If your head is hanging low today as mine has done on many a day, I hope you'll find the encouragement to know that you really only need to do one thing at this point — PERSIST. And that means taking just one step in the right direction — even a half step in the right direction.
Vic Johnson

812

When you're going through hell, keep on going.
Winston Churchill

813

It's always too early to quit.
Norman Vincent Peale

814

It's not that I'm so smart; it's just that I stay with problems longer.
Albert Einstein

815

The number one skill in life is not giving up.
Bryant McGill

816

Genius is one percent inspiration and ninety-nine percent perspiration.
Thomas A. Edison

817

If you give up at the first sign of struggle, you really aren't ready to be successful.

Kevin Hart

818

Persistence can change failure into extraordinary achievement.

Matt Biondi

819

People of mediocre ability sometimes achieve outstanding success because they don't know when to quit. Most men succeed because they are determined to.

George Allen

820

You just can't beat the person who never gives up.

Babe Ruth

821

If I had to pick one character trait that I think is a "must have" in order to be successful in any endeavor, it would be persistence. In fact, it seems to be the one trait that is the dominant trait in every single, super-successful individual I know. I believe it to be the one trait that any ordinary person can use to become extraordinary.

Vic Johnson

822

I'm not pushy, I'm professionally persistent.

Ursula Mentjes

823
It ain't over 'til it's over.
Yogi Berra

824
Don't watch the clock; do what it does. Keep going.
Sam Levenson

825
Our greatest weakness lies in giving up. The most certain way to succeed is to try just one more time.
Thomas A. Edison

826
No great thing is suddenly created.
Epictetus

827
Never give up. Great things take time.
Unknown

828
Success in life comes when you simply refuse to give up, with goals so strong that obstacles, failure, and loss only act as motivation.
Unknown

829
Don't be discouraged. It's often the last key in the bunch that opens the lock.
Unknown

830

She was unstoppable, not because she did not have failures or
doubts, but because she continued on despite them.
Beau Taplin

831

Great works are performed not by strength but by perseverance.
Samuel Johnson

832

Success doesn't happen overnight. Keep your prize and don't
look back.
Erin Andrews

833

You only fail when you stop trying.
Albert Einstein

834

I'm convinced that about half of what separates successful
entrepreneurs from the non successful ones is pure perseverance. .
. Unless you have a lot of passion about this, you're not going to
survive. You're going to give up.
Steve Jobs

835

Most of the important things in the world have been
accomplished by people who have kept on trying when there
seemed to be no hope at all.
Dale Carnegie

836
Never, never, never quit.
Winston Churchill

837
Many of life's failures are people who did not realize how close
they were to success when they gave up.
Thomas A. Edison

838
Persistent people begin their success where others end in failure.
Edward Eggleston

839
Let me look up into the branches of the towering oak and know
that it grew great and strong because it grew slowly and well.
Wilfred Peterson

840
We are made to persist. That's how we find out who we are.
Tobias Wolff

841
In the confrontation between the stream and the rock, the stream
always wins- not through strength but by perseverance.
H. Jackson Brown, Jr.

23.   Risk

842
The biggest risk is not taking any risk. In a world that's changing
really quickly, the only strategy guaranteed to fail is not taking
risks.
Mark Zuckerberg

843
The future belongs to the risk-takers, not the comfort-seekers.
Brian Tracy

844
If you're not willing to risk, you cannot grow. If you cannot grow,
you cannot be your best. IF you cannot be your best, you cannot
be happy. If you cannot be happy, what else is there?
Les Brown

845
Take risks. If you win, you'll be happy; if you lose, you'll be wise.
Unknown

846
The trouble is, if you don't risk anything, you risk even more.
Erica Jong

847
Unless you walk out into the unknown, the odds of making a
profound difference in your life are pretty low.
Tom Peters

848
By exposing yourself to risk, you're exposing yourself to heavy-duty learning, which gets you on all levels. It becomes a very emotional experience as well as an intellectual experience. Each time you make a mistake, you're learning from the school of hard knocks, which is the best education available.
Gifford Pinchot

849
You will either step forward into growth or you will step backward into safety.
Abraham Maslow

850
You can't play it safe your whole life and expect to reach your highest potential. You've got to be willing to take some risk.
Joel Osteen

851
The boat is safer anchored at the port; but that's not the aim of boats.
Paulo Coelho

852
Only those who will risk going too far can possibly find out how far one can go.
T. S. Eliot

24. Sales Success

853

You know you are running a modern sales team when selling feels more like the relationship between a doctor and a patient and less like a relationship between a salesperson and a prospect. When you go in to see your doctor and she asks you about your symptoms, you tell her the truth. You trust that she can diagnose your problem and prescribe the right medication. When she says, "This is what you have. Take these pills," you don't say, "Let me think about it" or "Can I get 20 percent off?" You take the medication. It's no longer about interrupting, pitching and closing. It is about listening, diagnosing and prescribing.
Mark Roberge

854

A person will not buy from you until he is convinced that you are a friend and are acting in his best interest. You must make that clear.
Brian Tracy

855

Value the relationship more than making your quota.
Jeffrey Gitomer

856

Internalize the Golden Rule of sales that says; All things being equal, people will do business with, and refer business to, those people they know, like and trust.
Bob Burg

857
There's no lotion or potion that will make sales faster and easier for you -unless your potion is hard work.
Jeffrey Gitomer

858
Sales comes from a Scandinavian word meaning "To Serve."
Deb Bixler

859
A smart salesperson listens to emotions not facts.
Zig Ziglar

860
Always think like doctor - never sell something until you find the pain. Don't talk about product/price until you find out pain.
Unknown

861
I am the world's worst salesman - therefore, I must make it easy for people to buy.
Franklin W. Woolworth

862
Life's too short to sell things you don't believe in.
Patrick Dixon

863
A good salesperson makes your customers problems your problems.
Unknown

864
The greatest sale you'll ever make is the right, privilege, honor and respect to meet with that person again.
Mark Hunter

865
A good salesman is one who can sell himself before selling his products.
Unknown

866
There is no prize in sales for second place. It's win or nothing. The masters know this and strive for - they fight for - that winning edge.
Jeffrey Gitomer

867
Make a habit of dominating the listening and let the customer dominate the talking.
Brian Tracy

868
All things being equal, people will do business with a friend; all things being unequal, people will still do business with a friend.
Mark McCormack

869
The key is not to call the decision maker. The key is to have the decision maker call you.
Jeffrey Gitomer

870
As a salesperson, you have all the power in the world to make your own success happen. It's not market conditions; it's your mental conditions. It's not customer conditions; it's your failure to perform in a powerful way. And it's certainly not the competition's conditions; it's your inability to prove value beyond doubt and risk.
Jeffrey Gitomer

871
Prospects equal options. Master prospecting and you will be the master of your sales destiny.
Tibor Shanto

872
Don't sell life insurance. Sell what life insurance can do.
Ben Feldman

873
People don't want to buy a quarter-inch drill. They want a quarter-inch hole!
Theodore Levitt

874
When the customer says "Yes"- STOP TALKING
Michael Bloomberg

875
In sales, a referral is the key to the door of resistance.
Bo Bennett

876
Nobody likes to be sold, but everybody likes to buy.
Earl Taylor

877
We don't make money when we sell things; we make money
when we help people make purchase decisions.
Jeff Bezos

878
Don't find customer for your products, find products for your
customers.
Seth Godin

879
In what order customer buys?
· First, you
· Then your products or services
· Last your company
Gerry Robert

880
Sell the problem you solve, not the product.
Unknown

881
The unanswered question of the ages is why are you out making
cold calls instead of earning referrals?
Jeffrey Gitomer

882
You don't close a sale, you open a relationship if you want to build a long-term, successful enterprise.
Patricia Fripp

883
If every customer refers you to one customer you never have to do marketing.
Eric Lofholm

884
Measure your success not on the level of profit you're making today, but on the level of the referrals you're getting today.
Mark Hunter

885
People don't ask for facts in making up their minds. They would rather have one good, soul-satisfying emotion than a dozen facts.
Robert Keith Leavitt

886
In our desire to prove how worthy and clever we are to our prospects and clients, we can talk our way out of a sale.
Sue Barrett

887
Most successful people focus their time and energy on high-probability buyers. Skip the others.
Nancy Bleeke

888
When you lose a sale, don't lose the lesson, too.
An old saying in sales

889
To succeed in sales, simply talk to lots of people every day. And here's what's exciting- there are lots of people!
Jim Rohn

890
Treat objections as requests for further information.
Brian Tracy

891
People rarely buy what they need. They buy what they want.
Seth Godin

892
Sell the products that are so good they sell themselves. Those are the ones you can believe in. And that's the key to a successful career in sales and marketing.
John Forde

893
If you make a sale, you can earn a commission. If you make a friend, you can earn a fortune.
Jeffrey Gitomer

894
Sales is leadership; leadership is sales. Do customers want to buy from a follower or a leader?
Mark Hunter

895

Value first, connections second, money third. Money is not the motive, it's the by-product and the report card for doing the right thing with value.
Jeffrey Gitomer

896

The sale begins when the customer says yes.
Harvey Mackay

897

There is no such thing as a no sale call. A sale is made on every call you make. Either you sell the client some stock or he sells you a reason he can't. Either way a sale is made, the only question is who is gonna close? You or him? Now be relentless, that's it, I'm done.
Jim Young

898

Expose yourself to new people. Trying to sell the same opportunity to the same people over and over will give you the same results.
Unknown

899

The prime strategy for getting your way is implementing a persuasion process that leads to a positive outcome.
Jeffrey Gitomer

900

It's not hard sell, it's heart sell. Good questions get to the heart of the problem/ need/situation very quickly - without the buyer feeling like he or she is being pushed.

Jeffrey Gitomer

901

Salespeople today ARE the differentiator. That's why it's so critical for you to focus on becoming a valuable business asset to your customers.

Jill Konrath

902

Quality questions create a quality life. Successful people ask better questions, and as a result, they get better answers.

Tony Robbins

903

The best salespeople know that their expertise can become their enemy in selling. At the moment they are tempted to tell the buyer what "he needs to do," they instead offer a story about a peer of the buyer.

Mike Bosworth

904

Your Money is in the Follow-up.

Unknown

905

Success in sales is the result of disciple, dedication and sacrifice.

Thomas Roy Cromwell

906
In sales, it's not what you say; it's how they perceive what you say.
Jeffrey Gitomer

907
The era of the one night stand is gone... the sale merely consummates the courtship, at which time the marriage begins.
Theodore Levitt

908
Your first words set the tone. All encounters with customers and prospects are yours to control. The first words you deliver set the tone for the encounter. What word and tone choices are you making?
Jeffrey Gitomer

909
Spend more time building rapport and qualifying and you'll spend less time overcoming objections!
Butch Bellah

910
Whatever you do, don't obsess over forecasting. Get out there and build your pipeline.
Dan Perry

911
You already know how to make every sale, you're just not using your own sales power.
Jeffrey Gitomer

912
A deal can always be made when the parties see it to their own benefit.
Harvey Mackay

913
Most marketers stop short of striking gold in their list, giving up too quickly on unconverted leads.
Dan Kennedy

914
As a novelist, I tell stories and people give me money. Then financial planners tell me stories and I give them money.
Martin Cruz Smith

915
Respect the customer's time but give them a compelling reason to speak with you.
Keith Rosen

916
The bane of every B2B sales pro is the false prospect—a prospect that's never going to become a customer.
Geoffrey James

917
Only take a lost sale personally when you made the relationship too personal too soon.
Leanne Hoagland Smith

918
If you can establish common ground with your prospects, they will like you, trust you, tell you the truth, and buy from you.
Jeffrey Gitomer

919
It is almost always true that the person with the best information is the person who wins the sale.
Kelly Riggs

920
I like to think of sales as the ability to gracefully persuade, not manipulate, a person or persons into a win-win situation.
Bo Bennett

921
Sales is all about having the commitment to serve and the passion to sell.
Mark Hunter

922
Stop selling. Start helping.
Zig Ziglar

923
To sell faster, be more disciplined in your approach to qualification, discovery, and all your core sales processes.
Andy Paul

924
The questions you ask are more important than the things you could ever say.
Tom Freese

925

You don't need a big close, as many sales reps believe. You risk losing your customer when you save all the good stuff for the end. Keep the customer actively involved throughout your presentation, and watch your results improve.
Harvey Mackay

926

I put myself in front of people who can say yes to me, and I deliver value first.
Jeffrey Gitomer

927

Sales leads are like lottery tickets. They won't all be winners, but you don't know until you engage.
Andy Paul

928

Ninety percent of selling is conviction and 10 percent is persuasion.
Shiv Khera

929

Leads are like a salad. The difference between salad and garbage is timing. Timing is everything.
Dan Kennedy

930

Set aside some time to review your calendar for the past 12 months, you might find someone you had forgotten to follow up with.
Ken Thoreson

931
Sales are contingent upon the attitude of the salesman, not the attitude of the prospect.
W. Clement Stone

932
You have to drop your sales mentality and start working with your prospects as if they've already hired you.
Jill Konrath

933
Nobody is going to buy from you have a quota to meet. They are going to buy from you because they see value in doing so.
Bob Burg

934
You can catch more flies with honey than with vinegar.
Old adage

935
Take more chances than you dare. You'll make more sales than you expect. That's the formula.
Jeffrey Gitomer

936
Sell, don't tell. When you're talking, you're not selling.
Robert Nadeau

937

There are two types of salespeople that enter a room—the first one walks in and says, 'Here I am!' The second one walks in and says, 'Ah, there you are!'
Brian Moran

938

I love working with customers. Sales has really influenced everything I do. It has instilled in me the important traits of operating with a sense of urgency and listening to people.
Jeffrey Gitomer

939

Selling to people who actually want to hear from you is more effective than interrupting stranger who don't.
Seth Godin

940

The first viable vendor in front of a hot prospect is five times more likely to win the sale.
Craig Elias

941

You've got to be success minded. You've got to feel that things are coming your way when you're out selling; otherwise, you won't be able to sell anything.
Benjamin Jowett

942

Buying motives are more powerful than selling skills. If you learn why people buy and your competition only knows how to sell, you won't just beat them, you'll bury them.
Jeffrey Gitomer

943
The less you focus on your motive to meet, the more likely it is that your connection will be successful. All connections need not be sales, but they can lead to sales. Is your focus short-term gain, or a long-term relationship?
Jeffrey Gitomer

944
Once a prospect has made the decision to make a purchase, he or she is in buying mode so to speak. They've got their wallet out and are looking to solve a problem or satisfy a need. When you offer them a better solution, they'll pay more. At least 30% of them will!
Charlie Cook

945
Discover their pain. Present the solutions!
Unknown

946
Buyer confidence must be established and reconfirmed in all phases of the selling process.
Jeffrey Gitomer

947
When reps "check-in" or "touch base" they're wasting everyone's time.
Unknown

948
Keep your sales pipeline full by prospecting continuously. Always have more people to see than you have time to see them.
Brian Tracy

949
Don't deliver a product. Deliver an experience.
Unknown

950
Prospects are making their purchase decision based on whether they think you understand their problems and you have the knowledge, resources and commitment to solve them.
Trish Bertuzzi

951
Call the leads that fell through the cracks. There's never a reason to let a lead pass you by.
Kendra Lee

952
The key in mastering any kind of sales is switching statements about you and how great you are and what you do, to statements about them, and how great they are and how they will produce more and profit more from ownership of your product or service.
Jeffrey Gitomer

953
Everyone has a story to tell or product to sell. Know your audience before you open your mouth.
Unknown

954
Every no brings me closer to a yes.
Mark Cuban

955

Sales is like cooking, you need to use the right ingredients, in the right quantities, at the right time and in the right order.
Hitesh Changela

956

Make your product easier to buy than your competition, or you will find customers buying from them, not you.
Mark Cuban

957

I have never worked a day in my life without selling. If I believe in something, I sell it, and I sell it hard.
Estée Lauder

958

Sales people should take lessons from their kids. What does the word 'no' mean to a child? Almost nothing.
Jim Rohn

959

Keep calm and close the deal.
Unknown

960

You have to generate revenue as efficiently as possible. And to do that, you must create a data-driven sales culture. Data trumps intuition.
Dave Elkington

961
Persuasion is an art. Never crossing the line to "pushy." It's showing reserve and poise. In short - being cool.
Jeffrey Gitomer

962
Selling is getting someone intellectually engaged in a future result that is good for them and getting them to emotionally commit to take action to achieve that result.
Dan Sullivan

963
The key to mastering any kind of sales is switching statements about you, how great you are, and what you do, to statements about them, and how great they are, and how they will produce more and profit more from ownership of your product or service.
Jeffrey Gitomer

964
Your customers do not buy because they're being marketed to or sold to. Instead, they buy because you help them realize the merits of owning what you offer.
Jay Conrad Levinson

965
For every sale you miss because you're too enthusiastic, you will miss a hundred because you're not enthusiastic enough.
Zig Ziglar

966
Creating the WOW! moment should be an objective within every sales cycle.
Unknown

967
When you're not getting rejections you just aren't selling enough.
Unknown

968
Follow up, follow up, follow up until they buy, die or tell you to go away.
Eric Lofholm

969
People want to do business with you because you HELP THEM get what they want. They don't do business with you to help YOU get what YOU want.
Don Crowther

970
The top salesperson in the organization probably missed more sales than 90% of the sales people on the team, but they also made more calls than the others made.
Zig Ziglar

971
It's about listening first, then selling.
Erik Qualman

972
When selling, never answer an unasked question.
Jeff Thull

973
You must learn that the key to selling is not selling; it is providing. And the key to providing is knowing in advance what to provide.
Todd Duncan

974
Average sales people pitch facts. Exceptional sales reps pitch visions.
Unknown

975
Become comfortable with silence. Don't talk while your customer is thinking about your offer.
Brian Tracy

976
Great salespeople listen 80% of the time and talk only 20% of the time.
Steve Keating

977
The sale most often goes to the most interested party.
Steve Chandler

978
Pretend that every single person you meet has a sign around his or her neck that says, 'Make me feel important.' Not only will you succeed in sales, you will succeed in life.
Mary Kay Ash

979
In firms that don't have a sales process, much relies on then a miracle happens.
Kevin Avery

980
Enchantment is the purest form of sales. Enchantment is all about changing people's hearts, minds and actions because you provide them a vision or a way to do things better. The difference between enchantment and simple sales is that with enchantment you have the other person's best interests at heart too.
Guy Kawasaki

981
Talk to 2 new people a day-700 a year - you will get more business than you can imagine.
Bill Bailey

982
Sales success comes after you stretch yourself past your limits on a daily basis.
Omar Periu

983
Some people fold after making one timid request. They quit too soon. Keep asking until you find the answers. In sales there are usually four or five "no's" before you get a "yes".
Jack Canfield

984
If I could live my life over again, I'd ask for bigger orders.
J. Paul Getty

985

Every sale has five basic obstacles: no need, no money, no hurry, no desire, no trust.
Zig Ziglar

986

Always be closing...That doesn't mean you're always closing the deal, but it does mean that you need to be always closing on the next step in the process.
Shane Gibson

987

If you walk in knowing what it will take to get their business, it's most likely you will walk out with the order.
Jeffrey Gitomer

988

You cannot bore people into buying your product; you can only interest them into buying it.
David Ogilvy

989

If you are not moving closer to what you want in sales (or in life), you probably aren't doing enough asking.
Jack Canfield

990

In selling as in medicine, prescription before diagnosis is malpractice.
Tony Alessandra

991
Top salespeople understand they must learn to feel comfortable doing the uncomfortable.
Tim Sales

992
Selling in its simplest form? Finding out what people want and helping them get it.
Unknown

993
In sales there are going to be times when you can't make everyone happy. Don't expect to and you won't be disappointed. Just do your best for each client in each situation as it arises. Then, learn from each situation how to do it better the next time.
Tom Hopkins

994
In the South, we tell stories. We tell stories if you're in a sales position, if you're in a retail position, you lure your customer by telling a story. You just do.
Tate Taylor

25.   Self Confidence

995

I don't like to gamble, but if there's one thing I'm willing to bet on, it's myself.

Beyoncé

996

The greatest pleasure in life is doing what people say you cannot do.

Walter Bagehot

997

People believe in those who believe in themselves. No one wants to be stuck in a room with other people who feel like they don't deserve to be there. Stop wondering if you're good enough. Know you are, and start acting like it.

Simon Black

998

Don't let someone else's opinion of you become your reality.

Les Brown

999

Best Thing I ever did was Believe in me.

Unknown

1000

Self-confidence is the first requisite to great undertakings.

Samuel Johnson

1001
Believe in yourself! Have faith in your abilities! Without a humble but reasonable confidence in your own powers you cannot be successful or happy.
Norman Vincent Peale

1002
You have within you right now. Everything you need to deal with whatever the world can throw at you.
Brian Tracy

1003
Our greatest weakness is lack of self-confidence.
Angela Ahrendts

1004
The most important sale in life is to sell yourself to yourself.
Maxwell Maltz

1005
There will be haters, there will be doubters, there will be non-believers, and then there will be you, proving them wrong.
Unknown

1006
Be yourself; everyone else is already taken.
Oscar Wilde

1007
Confidence and enthusiasm are the greatest sales producers in any kind of economy.
O. B. Smith

1008
When you have confidence, you can have a lot of fun. And when you have fun, you can do amazing things.
Joe Namath

1009
The man who has confidence in himself gains the confidence of others.
Hasidic Proverb

1010
Millions of people can believe in you, and yet none of it matters if you don't believe in yourself.
Unknown

1011
The world has the habit of making way for the man whose words and actions show that he knows where he is going.
Napoleon Hill

1012
Confidence is preparation. Everything else is beyond your control.
Richard Kline

1013
Whatever you believe about yourself on the inside is what you will manifest on the outside.
Unknown

1014
You have to pretend you're 100 percent sure. You have to take action; you can't hesitate or hedge your bets. Anything less will condemn your efforts to failure.
Andy Grove

1015
To be a great champion you must believe you are the best. If you're not, pretend you are.
Muhammad Ali

1016
Only make decisions that support your self-image, self-esteem, and self-worth.
Oprah Winfrey

1017
Believe in yourself and all that you are. Know that there is something inside you that is greater than any obstacle.
Christian D. Larson

1018
No one can make you feel inferior without your consent.
Eleanor Roosevelt

1019
The best way to sell yourself to others is first to sell the others to yourself.
Napoleon Hill

1020
To double your net worth, double your self-worth. Because you will never exceed the height of your self-image.
Robin Sharma

1021
Outstanding leaders go out of their way to boost the self-esteem of their personnel. If people believe in themselves, it's amazing what they can accomplish.
Sam Walton

1022
Make sure you don't start seeing yourself through the eyes of those who don't value you. Know your worth even if they don't.
Thema Davis

1023
Your self-worth is determined by you. You don't have to depend on someone to tell you who you are.
Beyoncé

1024
A tiger doesn't lose sleep over the opinion of sheep.
Unknown

1025
Success is liking yourself, liking what you do, and liking how you do it.
Maya Angelou

1026
One important key to success is self-confidence. An important key to self-confidence is preparation.
Arthur Ashe

1027
History will be kind to me for I intend to write it.
Winston Churchill

1028
Because believing that the dots will connect down the road will give you the confidence to follow your heart, even if it leads you off the well-worn path, and that will make the difference.
Steve Jobs

1029
Confidence is silent. Insecurities are loud.
Unknown

1030
Customers are buying confidence. It's up to us to show it.
Mark Hunter

1031
Your self-image controls your performance; see yourself as confident and in complete control.
Brian Tracy

1032
No one is you, and that is your power.
Dave Grohl

1033

Don't let fear or insecurity stop you from trying new things.
Believe in yourself. Do what you love. And most importantly, be
kind to others, even if you don't like them.
Stacy London

1034

Self-esteem and self-love are the opposites of fear; the more you
like yourself, the less you fear anything.
Brian Tracy

1035

Act as if what you do makes a difference. It does.
William James

1036

Many salespeople are trying to make their quota rather than
developing a deeper belief in their product or service - and even
worse, they don't have a strong enough belief in themselves.
Jeffrey Gitomer

1037

Believe you can & you're halfway there.
Theodore Roosevelt

1038

You are your greatest asset. Put your time, effort and money into
training, grooming, and encouraging your greatest asset.
Tom Hopkins

1039

You must expect great things of yourself before you can do them.
Michael Jordan

1040
Too many people undervalue what they are, and overvalue what they're not.
Malcolm Forbes

1041
I must undertake to love myself and to respect myself as though my very life depends upon self-image, love and self-respect.
Maya Angelou

1042
Jealousy is the result of one's lack of self-confidence, self-worth, and self-acceptance.
Sasha Azevedo

1043
We will either find a way or we will make one.
Hannibal

1044
People are going to judge you anyway. So forget everyone and be yourself.
Unknown

1045
Obstacles can't stop you. Problems can't stop you. Most of all, other people can't stop you. Only you can stop you.
Jeffrey Gitomer

1046
If you want to achieve greatness stop asking for permission.
Unknown

26. Selling

1047
The most important single skill you must develop for succeeding
in your own business is the ability to sell yourself and your
product to your customers.
Brian Tracy

1048
Sales is like learning to swim. You can read all the books you
want. Go through the motions on the side of the pool. You can
look great in the mirror. But eventually, if you want to learn to
swim, you're going to have to get wet.
Ian Brodie

1049
Unless your product is so revolutionary that people are willing to
line up at your door for it, you need to learn how to sell;
otherwise, your days as a business owner are numbered.
Brian Moran

1050
Timid salesmen have skinny kids.
Zig Ziglar

1051

And old Dave, he'd go up to his room, y'understand, put on his green velvet slippers---I'll never forget---and pick up his phone and call the buyers, and without ever leaving his room, at the age of eighty-four, he made his living. And when I say that, I realized that selling was the greatest career a man could want.
Arthur Ashe

1052

Best way to sell something: don't sell anything. Earn the awareness, respect, and trust of those who might buy.
Rand Fishkin

1053

People buy emotionally but defend their choice logically.
Jerry Acuff

1054

The sales department isn't the whole company, but the whole company better be the sales department.
Philip Kotler

1055

I have always said that everyone is in sales. Maybe you don't hold the title of salesperson, but if the business you are in requires you to deal with people, you, my friend, are in sales.
Zig Ziglar

1056

A good sales process should also be aligned with how buyers buy rather than with how salespeople want to sell.
Keith Eades

1057
Your challenge is to lead your prospects so they will follow you - and turn into customers.
Jeffrey Gitomer

1058
A salesman, like the storage battery in your car, is constantly discharging energy. Unless he is recharged at frequent intervals he soon runs dry. This is one of the greatest responsibilities of sales leadership.
R. H. Grant

1059
When you sell to someone at a business, it's worth remembering that the pain their problem is causing belongs to them, while the money they have to spend, doesn't.
Seth Godin

1060
The point to remember about selling things is that, as well as creating atmosphere and excitement around your products, you've got to know what you're selling.
Stuart Wilde

1061
Sales are the engine that pulls the train. Everything else follows.
Harvey Mackay

1062
Selling something is not the goal. Having someone WANT to buy what you have is the GOAL.
Larry Thompson

1063
One way to sell to a consumer in the future is simply to get his/her permission in advance.
Seth Godin

1064
You can have brilliant ideas but if you can't get them across, your ideas won't get you anywhere.
Lee Iacocca

1065
Some `authorities' say that selling is a job of the past. I say selling is the best job of the future. Customers need you more than ever, if you understand that they need help and they need caring. Trust-based transactions are the real deal, more than ever in the past.
Patrick Valtin

1066
Be a resource not a sales pitch.
Unknown

1067
Implement solutions, not features.
John Geleynse

1068
80% of sales are generated from 20% of your clients.
Pareto principle

1069

A sale is not something you pursue; it's what happens to you
while you are immersed in serving your customer.
Unknown

1070

As you travel down life's highway...whatever be your goal, you
cannot sell a doughnut without acknowledging the hole.
Harold J. Shayler

1071

In business, you're the Chief Salesman. Create a sense of
demand, rather than waiting to have demand.
Barbara Corcoran

1072

So long as new ideas are created, sales will continue to reach new
highs.
Dorothea Brande

1073

The most important sale is not the first sale; it is the second sale.
You can get the first sale with promises and price discounts, but
you can only get the second sale by satisfying your customer in
such a way that he prefers to buy from you again rather than buy
from someone else.
Brian Tracy

1074

To be successful in business you don't just need a great idea —
you have to sell it. Don't be afraid to sell. Don't think of yourself
as anything but a marketer.
Susan Sobbott

1075

I still work hard to know my business. I'm continuously looking for ways to improve all my companies, and I'm always selling. Always.
Mark Cuban

1076

Selling Is a Process, Not an Event.
Unknown

1077

Refuse to let the fear of rejection hold you back. Remember rejection is never personal.
Brian Tracy

1078

More has changed in selling in the past three years, than in the entire history of selling.
Dave Stein

1079

People do not buy goods and services. They buy relations, stories and magic.
Seth Godin

1080

To me, job titles don't matter. Everyone is in sales. It's the only way we stay in business.
Harvey Mackay

1081

Everyone makes their living by selling something to someone.
Robert Louis Stevenson

1082
Engaging people is about meeting their needs, not yours.
Tony Robbins

1083
I'm not good at selling laptops. I'm good at selling ideas.
Nicholas Negroponte

1084
Prospecting - Find the man with the problem.
Ben Friedman

27.   Success

1085
There is only one success - to be able to spend your life in your own way.
Christopher Morley

1086
The secret of success is to know something nobody else knows.
Aristotle Onassis

1087
Success is not the key to happiness. Happiness is the key to success. If you love what you are doing, you will be successful.
Albert Schweitzer

1088
Most people have the will to win, few have the will to prepare to win.
Bobby Knight

1089
Successful people are always looking for opportunities to help others. Unsuccessful people are always asking, 'what's in it for me?'
Brian Tracy

1090
The dictionary is the only place where success comes before work. Hard work is the price we must all pay for success.
Vince Lombardi

1091
The price of success must be paid in full, in advance.
Brian Tracy

1092
The elevator to success is out of order. You'll have to use the
stairs... One step at a time.
Joe Girard

1093
It is literally true that you can succeed best and quickest by
helping others to succeed.
Napoleon Hill

1094
The difference between a successful person and others is not a
lack of strength, not a lack of knowledge, but rather a lack of will.
Vince Lombardi

1095
A winner is someone who recognizes his God-given talents,
works his tail off to develop them into skills, and uses those skills
to accomplish his goals.
Larry Bird

1096
I attribute my success to this: I never gave or took any excuse.
Florence Nightingale

1097
Don't take rest after your first victory because if you fail in second, more lips are waiting to say that your first victory was just luck.
A.P.J. Abdul Kalam

1098
Success is no accident. It is hard work, perseverance, learning, studying, sacrifice and most of all, love of what you are doing or learning to do.
Pele

1099
If you do what you've always done, you'll get what you've always gotten.
Tony Robbins

1100
Success leaves clues. Go figure out what someone who was successful did, and model it. Improve it, but learn their steps. They have knowledge.
Tony Robbins

1101
One of the most important keys to success is having the discipline to do what you know you should do, even when you don't feel like doing it.
Unknown

1102
You're the average of the five people you spend most of your time with.
Jim Rohn

1103
You can't argue with success.
Proverbs

1104
Success is the sum of small efforts, repeated day in and day out.
Robert Collier

1105
The tendency to follow the path of least resistance guarantees
failure in life.
Brian Tracy

1106
I've found that luck is quite predictable. If you want more luck,
take more chances. Be more active. Show up more often.
Brian Tracy

1107
To be a champion, you have to learn to handle stress and
pressure. But if you've prepared mentally and physically, you
don't have to worry.
Harvey Mackay

1108
The way to succeed is to double your error rate.
Thomas J. Watson

1109
There is little success where there is little laughter.
Andrew Carnegie

1110
There is only one road to human greatness: through the school of hard knocks.
Albert Einstein

1111
A successful man is one who can lay a firm foundation with the bricks that others throw at him.
Sidney Greenberg

1112
He that is good for making excuses is seldom good for anything else.
Benjamin Franklin

1113
High expectations are the key to everything.
Sam Walton

1114
Think continually in terms of the rewards of success rather than the penalties of failure.
Brian Tracy

1115
Winners have simply formed the habit of doing things losers don't like to do.
Albert Gray

1116
Successful people never worry about what others are doing.
Unknown

1117
Success in life is not about luck, it is about managed thoughts, focused attention and deliberate action.
Trudy Vesotsky

1118
Success is not to be pursued; it is to be attracted by the person you become.
Jim Rohn

1119
Success - my nomination for the single most important ingredient is energy well directed.
Louis Lundborg

1120
If there is anything you want in life, find out how others have achieved it and then do the same things they did.
Brian Tracy

1121
The road to success is not a path you find but a trail you blaze.
Robert Breault

1122
Your success in life will be in direct proportion to what you do after you do what you are expected to do.
Brian Tracy

1123
Ego stops you from getting things done and getting people to work with you. That's why I firmly believe that ego and success are not compatible.
Harvey Mackay

1124
Winners lose much more often than losers. So if you keep losing but you're still trying, keep it up! You're right on track.
Matthew Keith Groves

1125
Small opportunities are often the beginning of great achievements.
Unknown

1126
Recipe for success: heat up an idea take action mix it up with passion and belief then add a dash of persistence.
Unknown

1127
To succeed you need something to hold on to; something to motivate you; something to inspire you.
Tony Dorsett

1128
At first they'll ask you why you're doing it. Later, they'll ask you how you did it.
Unknown

1129
Each success only buys an admission ticket to a more difficult problem.
Henry Kissinger

1130
The secret of man's success resides in his insight into the moods of people, and his tact in dealing with them.
J. G. Holland

1131
Some people succeed because they are destined to, but most people succeed because they are determined to.
Unknown

1132
To do more for the world than the world does for you - that is success.
Henry Ford

1133
The money I have is in direct proportion to the value I've given to others. The more I give of myself, incredibly, the more economic power comes my way.
Tod Barnhart

1134
There are no secrets to success. It is the result of preparation, hard work and learning from failure.
Colin Powell

1135
Success breeds complacency. Complacency breeds failure. Only the paranoid survive.
Andy Grove

1136
Winning isn't everything, but wanting to win is.
Vince Lombardi

1137
The person with the most flexibility has the best chance of achieving the outcome he or she desires.
Tony Jeary

1138
Whenever an individual or a business decides that success has been attained, progress stops.
Thomas J. Watson

1139
I am not judged by the number of times I fail. But the number of times I succeed. And the number of times I succeed is a direct proportion to the number of times I fail and keep trying.
Tom Hopkins

1140
Success is a journey, not a destination. The doing is often more important than the outcome.
Arthur Ashe

1141
Opportunities are never lost; they are taken by others.
Unknown

1142
Success depends upon previous preparation, and without such preparation there is sure to be failure.
Confucius

1143
Success is not measured by what you do compared to what somebody else does. Success is measured by what you do compared to what you are capable of doing.
Zig Ziglar

1144
A man can succeed at almost anything for which he has unlimited enthusiasm.
Charles Schwab

1145
Success leads to success:
Success is always a work in progress.
Success doesn't come to you - you go to it.
Success is a journey, not a destination. Focus on the process.
Some people dream about success... While others wake up and work hard at it.
Success is achieved and maintained by those who try and keep trying.
Everyday is a good day to SUCCEED!
It comes down to a simple question: What do you want out of life, and what are you willing to do for it?
Unknown

1146
Optimism is more associated with success and happiness than
any other quality.
Brian Tracy

1147
You can accomplish anything in life, provided that you do not
mind who gets the credit.
Harry S. Truman

28.   Vision, Goal and Dream

1148
It's not OVER until you win! Your dream is possible.
Les Brown

1149
What you get by achieving your goals is not as important as what you become by achieving your goals.
Henry David Thoreau

1150
No matter where you're from, your dreams are valid.
Lupita Nyong'o

1151
If you have built castles in the air, your work need not be lost; that is where they should be. Now put the foundations under them.
Henry David Thoreau

1152
If you want to live a happy life, tie it to a goal, not to people or objects.
Albert Einstein

1153
Choosing a goal and sticking to it changes everything.
Scott Reed

1154

When we set goals; they work in two ways, we work on them and they work on us.
Bob Moawad

1155

The future belongs to those who believe in the beauty of their dreams.
Eleanor Roosevelt

1156

The greater danger for most of us lies not in setting our aim too high and falling short, but in setting our aim too low, and achieving our mark.
Michelangelo

1157

Chase the vision, not the money, the money will end up following you.
Tony Hsieh

1158

If your dreams don't scare you they aren't big enough.
Ellen Johnson Sirleaf

1159

Are you action right now consistent with your vision, goals and dreams? If the answer is no, step up. Live consistently with your dreams.
Eric Lofholm

1160
Build your own dreams, or someone else will hire you to build theirs.
Farrah Gray

1161
Don't let life change you goals, because achieving your goals can change your life.
Unknown

1162
You see things; and you say "Why?" But I dream things that never were; and I say "Why not?"
George Bernard Shaw

1163
The tragedy in life doesn't lie in not reaching your goal. The tragedy lies in having no goal to reach.
Benjamin Mays

1164
Goals must never be from your ego, but problems that cry for a solution.
Robert H. Schuller

1165
Sometimes life is about risking everything for a dream no one can see but you.
Unknown

1166
The best vision is insight.
Malcolm Forbes

1167
Keep your goals in front of you, and your fears behind you.
Tony Robbins

1168
The best dreams happen when you're awake.
Cherie Gilderbloom

1169
Goals aren't enough. You need goals plus deadlines: goals big enough to get excited about and deadline to make you run. One isn't much good without the other, but together they can be tremendous.
Ben Feldman

1170
Don't let someone who gave up on their dreams talk you out of yours.
Unknown

1171
When obstacles arise, you change your direction to reach you goal; you do not change your decision to get there.
Zig Ziglar

1172
If you aren't getting rejected on a daily basis, then your goals aren't ambitious enough.
Chris Dixon

1173
GOALS are the links in the chain that connect activity to accomplishment.
Tom Ziglar

1174
All successful people are big dreamers. They image what their future could be, ideal in every respect, and then they work everyday toward their distant vision, that goal or purpose.
Brian Tracy

1175
Whatever the mind of man can conceive and believe, it can achieve.
Napoleon Hill

1176
Create the highest, grandest vision possible for your life, because you become what you believe.
Oprah Winfrey

1177
The only thing worse than being blind, is having sight but no vision.
Helen Keller

1178
The four Cs of making dreams come true: Curiosity, Courage, Consistency, Confidence.
Walt Disney

1179
The goal isn't more money. The goal is living life on your terms.
Chris Brogan

1180
Set high goals and standards for yourself; resist the temptation of
the comfort zone.
Brian Tracy

1181
Dreams come in a size too big so that we may grow into them.
Josie Bisset

1182
A goal without a plan is just a wish.
Antoine de Saint-Exupéry

1183
We must never stop dreaming. Dreams provide nourishment for
the soul, just as a meal does for the body.
Paulo Coelho

1184
Setting goals is the first step in turning the invisible into the
visible.
Tony Robbins

1185
Your ability to discipline yourself to set clear goals, and then to
work toward them every day, will do more to guarantee your
success than any other single factor.
Brian Tracy

1186
If you want to reach a goal, you must 'see the reaching' in your own mind before you actually arrive at your goal.
Zig Ziglar

1187
You can accomplish virtually anything if you want it badly enough and if you are willing to work long enough and hard enough.
Brian Tracy

1188
The bigger the dream the higher you go.
Unknown

1189
Begin with the end in mind.
Stephen Covey

1190
Don't be pushed by your problems. Be led by your dreams.
Ralph Waldo Emerson

1191
If you don't know where you're going any road will get you there.
Lewis Carroll

1192
Any goal can be accomplished if you break it down into enough small steps.
Henry Ford

1193
You must either modify your dreams or magnify your skills.
Jim Rohn

1194
Be stubborn about your goals, and flexible about you methods.
Unknown

1195
The two most important days in your life are the day you are born and the day you find out why.
Mark Twain

1196
You have to dream before your dreams can come true.
A.P.J. Abdul Kalam

1197
Ambition is the first step to success. The second step is action.
Unknown

1198
Go confidently in the direction of your dreams. Live the life you have imagined.
Henry David Thoreau

1199
Outstanding people have one thing in common: An absolute sense of mission.
Zig Ziglar

1200
Never let your memories be greater than your dream.
Doug Ivester

1201
Dreams only die, if you let them starve.
Unknown

Did you enjoy this book?

Did you like this book? Then please help me in following three ways.

1) Can you give your review on www.amazon.com by expressing your opinion about this book?
2) Can you recommend this book to your family, friends and business colleagues?
3) Can you buy this book and send as a gift to anyone whom you think could be useful?

Amazing advertising opportunity

Would you like to sponsor the special edition of this book just for you? You can place your AD at most prominent part of this book.

If you want to sponsor at least 100 or more books just send email to hitesh@hiteshchangela.com

Thank you for choosing this book.

Bonus1: 201 Extra Free Quotes

Would you like to receive an amazing 201 free extra quotes?

To grab your 201 extra quotes, click here:
http://www.hiteshchangela.com/extraquotes

Bonus2: Build your action plan

Are you inspired by this book?

However, there are no benefits until you take action. Nothing happens until you become proactive and take action.

I have created an action plan to help you getting excellence in business and life.

To grab your action plan, click here:
http://www.hiteshchangela.com/actionplan

Index by Category

Index by Author

Johann Wolfgang Goethe 241,399
John Barrows 231
John Brunner 574
John D. Rockefeller 771,808
John D. Rockefeller (Jr.) 218
John F. Kennedy 777
John Forde 892
John Geleynse 1067
John Holmes 503
John Lasseter 152
John Mason 657
John Maxwell 357
John Muir 451
John Wanamaker 122
John Wooden 226,641,667,732
Jonathan Ive 591
Joshua J. Marine 186
Josie Bisset 1181
Joyce Meyer 602,627,674
Julia Child 802
June Martin 269
Karen Lamb 18
Katherine Barchetti 273
Keith Eades 1056

Keith Rosen 915
Kelly Riggs 919
Ken Blanchard 316
Ken Hensley 492
Ken Robinson 91,800
Ken Thoreson 930
Ken Venturi 768

Kendra Lee 951
Kenneth H. Blanchard 548
Kevin Avery 979
Kevin Hart 817
Kim Somers Egelsee 394
Kobi Yamada 523
Lao Tzu 32,788

Larry Bird 1095
Larry Ellison 128,142
Larry Thompson 1062
Lauren Freedman 295
Leanne Hoagland Smith 917
Lee Holz 575
Lee Iacocca 109,161,325,1064
Lee Jampolsky 633
Les Brown 84,379,502,844,998,1148
Lewis Carroll 1191
Li Smith 50
Linda Sanford 299
LL Cool J 666
Loretta Young 516
Lou Gerstner 276,300
Lou Holtz 171,342,748
Louis L' Amour 398
Louis Lundborg 1119
Lowell Thomas 765
Lupita Nyong'o 1150
Lupytha Hermin 258
Mae Jemison 568
Mae West 30,572
Mahatma Gandhi
212,214,266,331,434,466,477
Malcolm Forbes 213,745,1040,1166
Mandy Hale 77,195
Marianne Williamson 458
Mario Andretti 642
Marjorie Pay Hinckley 335
Mark Cuban 954,956,1075
Mark Hunter
148,280,298,738,864,884,894,921,1030
Mark McCormack 868
Mark Roberge 853
Mark Sanborn 803
Mark Twain 21,595,608,1195
Mark Zuckerberg 842
Marshall Goldsmith 201
Martin Cruz Smith 914

Proverbs 187,1103
Qui-Gon Jinn 402
R. H. Grant 1058
Rabindranath Tagore 28
Ralph Marston 69,72,166
Ralph Waldo Emerson
19,215,242,431,484,550,776,1190
Rand Fishkin 1052
Ray Kroc 463
Richard Bach 698
Richard Branson 163,376,529,728
Richard Kline 1012

Rikki Rogers 260
Rita Mae Brown 328
Robert Anthony 208
Robert Breault 1121
Robert Collier 1104
Robert Frost 469
Robert H. Schuller 628,1164
Robert Ingersoll 505
Robert J Shiller 413
Robert Keith Leavitt 885
Robert Kiyosaki 735
Robert Louis Stevenson 462,1081
Robert Nadeau 936

Robert Tew 483
Robin Sharma 11,407,514,563,1020
Ron Karr 314,688
Ronald Reagan 147,329
Rosa Parks 512

Rosalynn Carter 541
Ross Perot 301
Rumi 90
Ryan Kahn 702
Sam Levenson 824
Sam Walton 272,307,1021,1113

Samuel Beckett 671
Samuel Johnson 237,831,1000
SAP Ad 281
Sasha Azevedo 1042
Scott Adams 158
Scott Cook 141

Scott McNealy 324
Scott Reed 1153
Seneca 249,704
Serena Williams 416
Seth Godin
125,130,132,227,292,382,456,878,891,9
39,1059,1063,1079
Shane Gibson 986
Sheryl Pattek 270,304
Sheryl Sandberg 31,539
Shiv Khera 928
Sidney Greenberg 1111
Simon Black 997
Simon Sinek 123
Socrates 339,573
Sonia Ricotti 96
Sr. Thomas Watson 105
St Jerome 653
Stacy London 1033
Stephen Covey
217,326,409,552,601,614,752,1189
Stephen McCranie 359
Steve Ballmer 143
Steve Chandler 977
Steve James 286
Steve Jobs
108,126,207,274,439,631,834,1028
Steve Keating 976
Steve Maraboli 38,593
Stuart Wilde 1060
Sue Barrett 886
Sun Tzu 205
Susan Sobbott 1074

ABOUT HITESH CHANGELA

Hitesh Changela is CEO of CRM Ultimate Limited, an innovative software technology company, based in the UK. He helps small to medium size businesses by increasing their efficiency and sales. He makes it easier for businesses to create, track and keep customers for longer periods of time, if not for life.

Hitesh has worked in the IT industry for more than 16 years, including over 6 years at Microsoft Ireland. Through SDL, he worked on projects for multinationals such as IBM, Intel, HP, Canon, CA, Research in Motion and Vivendi.

Hitesh is a voluntary management consultant with social-spiritual, non-profit educational organisations to provide consultancy as well as leadership and management training. He also advises on strategic planning, organisation structure and event management.

He holds an MBA in Marketing.

Hitesh lives in London, UK.

You can visit his website at **www.hiteshchangela.com**

ABOUT CRM ULTIMATE, a CRM Software Company

We met our first client in June 2012. Even though they were using one of the top multinational CRM vendors for managing customers, they felt that only 10% of the programs functionality was applicable to them.

They asked us for our help. We knew through market research that other small business owners were facing the same problem. We, therefore, decided to develop a Customer Relationship Management (CRM) program.

This led us to develop CRMUltimate. We have since spent more than 17,000 development hours in shaping CRMUltimate.

We now stand as an innovative software technology company, based in the UK, with the sole aim of helping small to medium size businesses to increase their efficiency and ultimately their sales.

Our team has over 30 years' experience and all of our staff are highly qualified, having an MBA (Marketing) and Computer Software Engineering qualifications.

We understand that all businesses are unique and we treat them that way. We work closely with all our clients to understand their needs, fine-tune our CRM software and empower them with training and ongoing support so that they get the most out of using CRMUltimate.

Peter Drucker, the father of modern management, observed. "The purpose of business is to create and keep a customer."

That was our reasoning behind creating CRMUltimate: make it easier for businesses to create, track and keep customers for longer periods of time, if not for life.

Sign up for 14 days free trial at
http://www.CRMUltimate.com/trial

Workshop

Breakthrough Customer Growth
Get a clear roadmap to turbo-charge top line growth

This workshop is for you if you want to:

- Get even more new customers and generate even more sales from existing customers
- Identify and explore various ways to acquire a customer
- Know why customers prefer to do business with you
- Identify your best customers and get more customers through referral
- Build even more personal relationships with customers, thereby building customer loyalty and minimise customer loss
- Define and develop lead management and sales processes to achieve predictable sales
- Support your customers to the optimum
- Identify and track over 40 KPIs (Key Performance Indicators) for sales, marketing, service, customer and sales persons
- Discover various tools to make your company even more productive and profitable

Who Should Attend

Anybody from SME Businesses who are

- SME Business Owners or Managing Directors
- Sales and Marketing Directors/Managers
- Salespeople
- Marketing team
- Customer Service Reps/personnel
- Any customer-facing staff

Overview/Topics

1. Customer information

2. Marketing

3. Lead Management

4. Unconverted Leads

5. Lost Business

6. More Sales

7. Best Customers

8. Referral

9. Follow-up

10. Customer relationship

11. Customer Service

12. Sales Representative Management

13. Selling is a Process

14. Business Intelligence

15. Miscellaneous Tools

I guarantee that by the end of this workshop, you will have a Clarity, Tools and Technique more than 99% of business people out there.

Visit **http://hiteshchangela.com/workshop** for more information.

Upcoming book!

Breakthrough Customer Growth
15 proven ways to grow sales swiftly and effectively

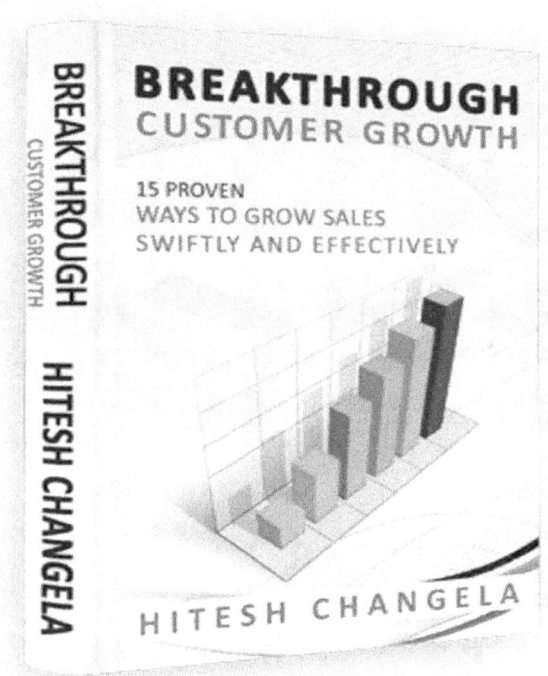

Why is the book unique?

The book focuses purely on how to generate sales from new and existing customers using CRM, to allow businesses to undergo sales transformation.

Unique features include:

- 184 ways to achieve sales using CRM.
- 214 actions or questions to help businesses generate even more sales.
- 67 fascinating facts.
- More than 110 mind-boggling quotes related to a particular chapter.
- 47 potential lead sources.
- 38 possible reasons a customer does business with you.
- 42 attributes/criteria by which your customers can rate your company.
- 26 communication methods you can use with your customers.
- 22 customer service attributes to check how satisfied your customers are.
- 24 sales team attributes to check how satisfied your customers are.

Any single idea, action, quote or fact mentioned in the book has a potential to transform your business.

More information, please visit
http://www.hiteshchangela.com/CRMbook

www.ingramcontent.com/pod-product-compliance
Lightning Source LLC
Chambersburg PA
CBHW060617290526
45793CB00001B/61